HEART

Experiencing the Fierce Love of the King

JANETTE WEHRMANN

WESTBOW
PRESS®
A DIVISION OF THOMAS NELSON
& ZONDERVAN

WestBow Press books may be ordered through booksellers or by contacting:

WestBow Press
A Division of Thomas Nelson & Zondervan
1663 Liberty Drive
Bloomington, IN 47403
www.westbowpress.com
844-714-3454

ISBN: 978-1-6642-5584-5 (sc)
ISBN: 978-1-6642-5586-9 (hc)
ISBN: 978-1-6642-5585-2 (e)

Library of Congress Control Number: 2022901025

Print information available on the last page.

WestBow Press rev. date: 02/21/2022

Dedication

For Jesus, who fiercely loves the world.
To my husband, Walt.
You have been a living example of Christ's love and forgiveness.
I am ever so grateful to our Lord Jesus Christ
for you, our children, all that He's done, doing and will do.

Dedication

Contents

Preface

This book is my testimony. It contains the true accounts of the most recent season in my life's journey with Jesus through His Holy Spirit. Having accepted and getting to know Jesus Christ as my Lord and Savior, is not a religious act. It's a real relationship, like a marriage, with all of life's joys and pains. Unlike a mortal, earthly marriage between a man and a woman, Jesus is always faithful and true. He's already forgiven me of all my mistakes and sin, therefore He's *always* ready to accept me when I acknowledge my poor behavior and incorrect way of thinking. He knows my deepest feelings, desires and thoughts. When I fail, He never does as Jesus is always faithful. He's perfect because He is God. God was in human flesh, died in human flesh and rose again, just as He said. Jesus did not rise from the dead in an earthly, humanly flesh body, but a supernatural one. (Acts 1:3-5, AMPC) God is Spirit, God is Love and God is Truth.

> "Now the Lord is the Spirit, and where the Spirit
> of the Lord is, there is liberty [emancipation
> from bondage, true freedom]."
> 2 Corinthians 3:17(AMP)

My desire is for you, the reader, to grasp hold of the Truth as you come to understand, relative to my experiences, the fierce Love Jesus has for you. Despite what you think or heard, what you have been through, what has been done to you or what you've done, the truth is He *fiercely* loves you and wants to have an eternal relationship with you. Similar as a father or husband should be, the Holy Spirit wants to love and protect you. He will provide you with everything you need and more. Like a helper/counselor, He will guide you and teach you the right way to live successfully on earth, with peace as you trust Him. Finally, Jesus Christ, not only as your Savior and Lord, but as King, like a husband or leader, He needs to be respected and not taken for granted, and He has the last "say so." He is sovereign, holy and just.

Will you accept His proposal? Will you allow Him to show you His love? I sincerely hope you will.

Fiercely Loved,
Janette Wehrmann

Acknowledgment

Jan Phares, thank you for answering the call and for your patience, kindness, and understanding during your assistance in editing this book. "You get me."

Included are many more friends, acquaintances, and others the Lord led me to, who have spoken encouraging words, words of life, which kept me motivated to finish the task of completing this book. This is for you. May the Lord bless you exceedingly as you keep Him centered in your life and may He be glorified.

Finally, to my husband, Walt, for your spiritual, moral, and loving support, with patience and long-suffering, as you are with many of my projects. I appreciate and love you.

Introduction

I am the eldest of three daughters, born and raised in Southern California. I have the privilege of inheriting a lineage of God-fearing relatives, some ministers of the Gospel. Walt and I met in Costa Mesa, California while attending college and were married in 1989. We have four children, three beautiful granddaughters and a wonderful grandson scheduled to be born February 15, 2022.

Our family's journey took us from the coastal region to the inland areas, up to the high desert, then back to the coastal area of Newport Beach, California. Sometimes I wondered if this experience was similar to Abraham's journey mentioned in the Holy Bible. As our boys grew and left our home, Walt and I were becoming empty nesters, having only Teagan, our youngest child and only daughter with us. Challenges were confronting us to move during Teagan's freshman year of high school, so Walt and I decided to return to Costa Mesa/Newport Beach. We recognized Teagan spent most of her life in the high desert. Although it was familiar to her, we discussed our plans to move, and she agreed and was excited to make new friends at a new school and live by the beach. We wanted to give our daughter a better life with more opportunities.

Unfortunately, the challenges we were confronted with followed us to Newport Beach, which made our move and living arrangements unpleasant. The hope we had for Teagan, for her to enjoy the remaining years of high school were somber. Not having all the members of her family together under one roof made this season more difficult and lonelier for our daughter. None-the-less, Walt and I continued to encourage her, love her, and keep her close to us.

Teagan successfully graduated from high school. Amidst the hardships endured, she overcame them by learning to depend on God and was well on her way to a new chapter in life. Just when we thought the new chapter in our lives was going to be promising, the devastation hit.

This is my story of what our family endured, how we overcame circumstances, and how we came to forgive.

I hope you will see and be blessed.

—Janette

"O taste and see that the LORD is good:
Blessed is the man that trusteth in him." Psalm 34:8 (KJV)

One
The Fourth Watch

Now the Lord came and stood and called
as at other times, "Samuel! Samuel!"
And Samuel answered, "Speak, for Your servant hears."
—1 Samuel 3:10 (NKJV)

It was just after three o'clock in the morning, perhaps a slight bit after, when I was startled awake from a dead sleep. *Where is Teagan?* I immediately jostled my husband and said, "Call her." We were so glad she answered her phone!

"Hello, Daddy. Yes, Daddy. I'm sorry, Daddy. I just have to take my friend home first, and then I'll come home. I love you, Daddy."

I could hear every word Teagan spoke since I was listening to the phone while snuggled right next to my husband. Hearing our daughter's voice gave me a peace, knowing she was safe and on her way home.

For some reason we both went back to sleep. I didn't wait up for Teagan to get home. I don't know why, but we soundly fell back asleep.

It must have been near 9:30 a.m. and our phones suddenly were abuzz with calls and messages from one of our elder sons, Zach. There had also been pounding at our door, but we didn't hear it. Finally, at approximately 10:00 a.m., we responded to Zach's call exclaiming, "Teagan's in the hospital!"

My husband, Walt, and I leaped out of bed and rushed to throw on whatever clothes we could grab quickly. Our call with Zach was full of questions. "Is she OK? What happened?" The next thing I knew, Walt and I jumped in our car and raced to UCI Medical Center in the city of Orange. My mind was spinning out of control with various frightening and tragic thoughts. And at the same time, I silently asked the Lord, "What's happening? Please let her be OK!" Walt and I were silent during most of the drive, approximately a twenty-five-minute journey. Holding my hand tightly, he said, "We're going to get through this together."

After his comment, the first thought that entered my mind was *What do you mean? Of course we're going to get through this together.* There was no doubt in my mind, and no other option. There never has been. It has always been us *together.*

When we arrived at the hospital, we immediately asked for Teagan Wehrmann. The staff didn't know her name. They called her Sugar Doe. *Sugar Doe?* I thought. The person who called Teagan Sugar Doe must have been a pleasant, older lady. I imagined the lady must have been a grandmother. Certainly, she must have seen Teagan's sweet face and her broken little body and, affectionately loving on Teagan, called her first name Sugar and last name Doe. It is common to call the unidentifiable Jane Doe. However, not my Teagan. The staff must have seen her preciousness through the eyes of our loving Lord Jesus and named her Sugar Doe.

Finally, they identified her and connected us as her parents, somewhat relieved after they had been looking for the closest relatives. We were informed that Teagan was in surgery. I said, "Surgery, what surgery?"

The person at the front desk couldn't or didn't have the authority to explain details thoroughly. She did, however, say this was Teagan's *second* surgery and she would be out soon. My heart was pounding while my mind was absolutely racing and questioning, *Second surgery? Why such a long time in surgery? What are they doing?*

Unanswered questions left our minds wondering. With mixed emotions, Walt and I were in a state of confusion and helplessly forced to wait. As my inward body started to churn and my heart ached, in my mind, I was asking the Lord, "What, Lord? What is it? What's going on? What can we do?" Thus, we waited.

Waiting is the most painful thing any person in this situation can endure because minds wander in opposite, disjointed directions. At least mine did. But as we waited, I also prayed. I prayed for the surgeons, the nurses, and whoever else was trying to help my daughter. I pleaded with the Lord to please heal her completely.

Now, Walt's been in some gnarly car accidents, yet I have never experienced life-threatening accidents. Walt is familiar with several medical terms and knows vital parts of the body and how they function. I'm not well versed and never wanted to be. Blood, broken bones, and such have never been my thing. I have always respected that tendency, and it has always respected me.

Finally, a staff member at the hospital called us. Zach had arrived at the hospital by then. Similarly, our son has had his share of experiences at different hospitals for various reasons throughout his life. Like his dad, he's intrigued how the human anatomy functions and is familiar with the terminology since Zach was taking biology courses in college. Wanting to protect his parents, Zach went first to observe his sister's condition and presentation from surgery. He spoke with nurses and gleaned more information regarding Teagan's condition. I didn't know what to expect, so I braced myself for the worst.

Looking back to the specific time of Teagan's accident, I started to wonder and asked myself, "Why at 3:30 a.m. on February 15?" The wondering led me to a memory of a particular movie I had watched with Walt one night, about the year 2005. I don't care for entertaining my mind with horror movies, but for some reason, the part of the movie that stuck with me was the acknowledgment the movie made of the spiritual activity that happened after 3:00 a.m. If I remember correctly, this unique film was made from a true account.

A few years passed after watching that "3:00 a.m. movie" when I stumbled upon an evangelist speaking about this matter on television. He was asking questions, rhetorically speaking, but I sensed his questions were directed toward me. As I answered *yes* in my mind, he went on to explain his own experiences, and I was thrown back by the similarities of my own accounts. Without going into detail, the evangelist confirmed and affirmed not only what we both personally experienced, but several accounts that were made in the Bible.

From then on, I learned of the significance regarding the fourth watch, which is defined by the Roman soldiers' watch time spanning from 3:00 a.m. to 6:00 a.m. Biblically, strategic events take place during these particular early morning watches or hours. Some of my favorite examples were found in the following:

- Genesis 32:22–31 (NKJV). In this account, Jacob wrestled with God, seeing Him face-to-face before receiving his blessing and entering his destiny as Israel. Verse 24 indicates the time when this occurred. "Then Jacob was left alone; and a Man wrestled with him until the breaking of day."
- Exodus 14:20–31 (AMPC). Before crossing the Red Sea, the Angel of God (Jesus), as a cloud, protected the Israelites by

coming between them and the Egyptians. Verse 24 states, "And in the morning watch the Lord through the pillar of fire and cloud looked down on the host of the Egyptians and discomfited [them]."

- And the one I love the most is found in Matthew 28:1 (NKJV). "Now after the Sabbath, as the first day of the week began to dawn, Mary Magdalene and the other Mary came to see the tomb."

The questions and some of the accounts the evangelist was referring to were of a strategic prayer time when woken/called by the Lord during the fourth watch, before dawn. Similar to 1 Samuel 3 when little Samuel first learned to recognize the Lord's voice calling him to prophesy to Eli, I too had to learn the voice of the Lord calling me, awakening me to pray early in the morning. I had to learn to say to the Lord, "Speak, for your servant hears" (verse 10 NKJV). I had to learn to *respond* to His calling. Like a parent calls out to their child and the child, most likely, should respond, "Yes?" it is no different when our heavenly Father calls us.

Those who have accepted Christ as their Lord and Savior are subject to God's call. But don't worry. Not everyone is called to wake up and pray in the middle of the night. God loves us all the same, but we have different destinies, talents, strengths, and callings. It would behoove us to willingly and obediently respond to His voice.

Looking back, this is why I couldn't understand the reasoning for going back into a deep sleep early that morning after hearing Walt speak with Teagan to come home. I sensed something was out of my control, like God was saying, "Janette, I've got this. Trust Me."

Two
The Little Window

♡

For God so loved the world that He gave His only begotten
Son, that whoever believes in Him should not perish
but have everlasting life. For God did not send His
Son into the world to condemn the world,
but that the world through Him might be saved.
—John 3:16–17 (NKJV)

A s we walked from the first-floor waiting area to the elevators,
my heart was pounding. When we exited the elevator to the
ICU ward, the nurse instructed us to wait in a tiny, private waiting
room. By this time, our youngest son, Tyler, and my mother had a
notification to come to the hospital. It took a few hours for Tyler
to reach the hospital because he lived a couple of hours away and
was working. Teagan's eldest brother, Jared, was in Turkey on an
army deployment. Jared was due to come home within weeks of the
accident. Teagan is our youngest and only daughter, and she has
three older brothers. Before being permitted into the ICU, the only
family members in the waiting room were Walt, Zach, my mother,
and me. It felt as though we had been there for a long time.

Finally, a police officer who was the head detective came in and shared information about the accident and asked questions about Teagan. He informed us that Teagan had been driving someone home at the time of the accident. He revealed who the passenger was. The passenger was Teagan's friend, Anthony. He was physically OK but undergoing observation for his wounds at the same hospital. Trying to be sensitive, the officer went into more details about the accident. He gingerly described the accident as one of the worst scenes the city of Huntington Beach has encountered. Then, he went on to say that Teagan was ejected from the vehicle upon impact from a drunk driver hitting the driver's side of the truck. The force was so hard that it severed a utility pole and caused a shut-down of the entire intersection for many hours. Teagan's belongings in the pick-up bed, locked down with a covered top, were scattered throughout the street. Police officers roped off the entire area and brought in a crew to pick up all her belongings and investigate the accident scene.

Additionally, the police detective warned us of legal obligations concerning the matter. Any legal issues he mentioned were the furthest things from my mind. Stuff or material things can be replaced, and bills can be paid. But our daughter? Our one-and-only precious daughter? What about the value of *her* life? A person's life is more valuable than stuff. No matter who that person is. Teagan was only five months into her nineteenth year of living, starting a new chapter in her life at college!

Questions were rolling through my head. *Will her body respond to the operations and heal properly? What if they do not solve her injuries? What will her care entail? Will she be able to play her instruments, drive a car again, or ride a motorcycle? How about walking, eating, or breathing? Will she be able to dance with her daddy on her wedding day? Will we be able to see her graduate from college? Will she be able to have children? What about our grandbabies?* These questions were churning, literally screaming inside my head as my heart felt incredibly heavy.

We waited yet further in the little room so the doctors could give us information concerning Teagan's condition. A young lady dressed in a surgical gown entered the room, asking for the parents of Teagan Wehrmann. At that point, I was sitting on the right side of Walt, where there was a corner table with a tissue box and a fake plant sitting on it. The young lady was part of the surgical team, and when she came into the room, she asked us again if we were Teagan's parents. I don't recall precisely how the young female doctor started the conversation, but she described a sequence of procedures they had performed on Teagan. The medical team removed Teagan's spleen and was overly concerned about her brain not responding. As my thoughts were tumultuous, filled with questions about the medical procedures and terminology and what it meant for Teagan, I could not comprehend what they told me. Plain and simple, I just wanted to see my daughter, and I wanted her to be OK.

Still sitting in my chair, I looked up and noticed a small window just as the young doctor finished her statements. There were four panes within the window, and the combination of them held together was a wooden frame that formed a cross. At that moment, I could feel what I had to do was kneel at the foot of that cross. Although my physical body was in a sitting position, my heart was utterly prostrate. I asked; I beseeched Jesus to tell me that my daughter was healthy and to please tell me what was going on! As I gazed at that little cross in the window, I then fell to my knees and wept, knowing what Jesus did at the cross. He could save my daughter and make her complete and whole.

Recently, I heard testimonies of people healed from their infirmities or dying and risen to live again. There are countless stories of Jesus performing miracles in the Bible, including raising people from the dead; ultimately, Christ himself rose from the grave. So I know that He can do it! But will He?

As I looked up at the little cross again, I didn't hear or pay attention to what people were talking about nor what they were doing. I felt like I was at a different level of understanding, as if my eyes were wide open to see, expect, and receive all that Christ was doing during this event. With all my questions and thoughts swirling in my head, my heart went out to my husband, our boys, and my daughter's friend, Anthony, who was lying in the hospital with his wounds and family at his side. Unexplainably, my heart swelled with deep compassion as I felt empathy for Teagan, Anthony, and those who were suffering around me. With my mind, I immediately asked the Lord, *Did she experience or endure great pain?* I never want my children to suffer any pain, although tribulation is inevitable. I've always disliked the times when they were hurting either emotionally or physically. By no means do I want my children to go through the pain I'm experiencing now nor what I had to endure during my lifetime.

I believe God loves us so much He never wanted us to go through pain. Genesis 2:16,17 (AMPC) reads, "And the Lord God commanded the man (Adam), saying, you may freely eat of every tree of the garden; But of the tree of knowledge of good and evil and blessing and calamity you shall not eat, for in the day that you eat of it you shall surely die." This passage tells me a few things:

- God gave man the freedom to eat from every tree except the one that would harm him. Isn't this like a loving parent? To place boundaries so that our children would not get hurt and bring pain or calamity to their lives?
- God warned him of the consequences; good and evil, blessing and calamity.
- God gave the man a choice. Life or death.

Scripture tells us in Genesis 2:9 (AMPC) "And out of the ground the Lord God made to grow every tree that is pleasant to the sight or to be desired—good (suitable, pleasant) for food; the tree of life also in the center of the garden, and the tree of the knowledge of [the difference between] good and evil and blessing and calamity."

Imagine if Adam and Eve ate from the tree of life? I believe there would be no sin, and we would be enjoying and living in God's eternal garden, in His presence with no sorrow and pain.

Unfortunately, the man chose death (ultimately). Adam disobeyed God. But thank goodness, God had a plan. His plan was the final, perfect sacrifice that would save the world from their sins and bring us back into a kindred relationship with Himself once again.

> "For the Son of Man came to seek and
> to save that which was lost."
> Luke 19:10 (AMPC)

I recalled the story of Jesus' suffering, suffering for us, the sin of the world, as I looked up at that little window cross. I remembered reading His Word, which said that He sacrificed Himself because He loves us. I wonder how Mary, the mother of Jesus, felt and thought, seeing her son, the Savior of the world, suffering. My heart and mind couldn't fathom the humiliation Jesus went through. The physical flogging, the horrible words they called Him, the mental, emotional, and physical pain Jesus endured because of His GREAT love for us. Over time, I realized some of the lavished mercy and grace He has given to my family, which came at such a significant cost.

I felt as if I was in a different dimension during the moment of my new revelation of experiencing the extraordinary indescribable love of Jesus, which was surreal and beyond wonderful. It was a bittersweet moment as I was agonizing over the thought of losing Teagan.

I felt such an overwhelming love that this body of mine could not contain it. I not only felt enveloped by it, but it permeated within me and flowed through me. It was uncontainable and unfathomable. I have never experienced anything like this. No words could describe this beautiful dense presence.

While receiving all of the love the Lord was allowing me to experience, somebody abruptly removed me from the peace that transcends all understanding back to reality. My mother exclaimed, "It's like Job!" Hearing her voice at that particular moment welling up inside me was an irritating feeling, and my thought was, *What is wrong with this woman? Is she unaware and not sharing my family's pain?* Raising my voice with an authoritative tone, I said, "Not now, mom!" When my mother is in a room, as sure as the sun rises, it seems like her need to share an unfiltered thought is customary. My experience has been of her consistently having an opinion to share. She will share when not invited or without regard for another family member's feelings as if she is entitled to disrespect because she's a mother. Instantly, I was taken back in time to many negative instances I had encountered with my mother growing up. Including the nonsense I had endured at her hands during the first 18 years of my marriage. Unfortunately, she has allowed herself to respond in the flesh by blurting out feelings or comments at the wrong time or setting, rather than using the fruit of self-control and being led by the Holy Spirit. These encounters have taught me several things:

- Sometimes, the enemy will try to use people to discourage us or get under our skin, which will tempt us to make us sin or think evil thoughts. It is especially true when you have a history with someone—usually a family member.

Instantly, I had to remind the devil that I was no longer in bondage and blind to his tactics. My mother's typical behavior was just a red flag of spiritual warfare. My soul's enemy was trying to get under my skin, thus making me feel and think horrible things about myself as they did in my past. God's Word teaches us that we do not war against flesh and blood, i.e., my mother, but against the spirits of darkness and the forces of evil.

> "For we do not wrestle against flesh and blood, but against
> principalities, against powers, against the rulers of the
> darkness of this age, against spiritual hosts of wickedness
> in the heavenly places." Ephesians 6:12. (NKJV)

- The other is: But, God. Sometimes, God may be trying to tell us something if and when we pay attention. Even though my mother used impeccable timing, what she said was not necessarily wrong or hurtful; "It's like Job!" That statement could have only been from my loving Lord, not my mother. So, I pondered that statement and tabled it for another time. Another time to learn whatever God wants me to know and understand of Him. To be closer to Him.

Quickly I turned my mind and heart back to the cross. I felt such peace as I returned my focus to the astounding love I was experiencing. I refused to let anything or anyone disengage me from the presence of the Lord, and His fierce Love, which He graciously indwelled in me. I desperately longed to see my daughter, to hold her and let her know that I was there. I wanted to assure her that everything would be OK. I wanted to shout that God is on His throne and has everything under control! Was I speaking to myself? Was I trying to convince myself, my husband, our sons, or Teagan?

After the briefing with Teagan's doctor, it was time to see her. As Walt and I walked from the tiny waiting room through the ICU hallway doors, hand-in-hand, I noticed the left side was a nurse's station, and on the right side, there were rows of rooms. I glanced in not to be obtrusive, but it was merely a reaction. I either saw patients lying motionless with nurses attending them or loved ones with bereaved worried faces, waiting for their loved ones to respond. My heart was racing from not knowing the condition I would see my daughter in. When we approached her room, directly across from the nurse's station, the curtain near her bed was drawn so Teagan could not be seen. We cautiously peeked in, carefully approaching the bed where she was lying. Our one-and-only baby girl was hooked up to all types of machines as she was fighting for her life.

Three
The Promise

The Lord is near to all who call upon Him,
To all who call upon Him in truth.
He will fulfill the desire of those who fear Him;
He also will hear their cry and save them.
—Psalms 145:18–19 (NKJV)

As our baby was lying lifeless in the hospital bed, I started to reflect on our past. Amid my spirit sensing such great love, I yearned to have good thoughts of our daughter, although mixed with deep emotional pain. I was determined not to forget and hold on to all memories and experiences with our daughter Teagan.

During our early years of marriage, I worked for a microfilm company when I felt the Lord calling me to stay home. I felt Him wooing me every day on my way to work as I listened to a Christian radio station. Inspirational pastors or Christian leaders discussed cultural matters, comparing them to God's Word. The only time I could fill myself spiritually, feeding on God's truth, was during my commute. I was too busy working during the day, and in the evenings while my husband either went to school or worked, I took care of our two beautiful and very healthy, active boys. I remember feeling refreshed, loved, and strengthened during those twenty-minute drives to the office. I thank the Lord for Christian broadcasts! We didn't have the luxury of podcasts or iHeart radio in the early '90s. The inspiration I received from the Word during Sunday church services only remained with me about half the day because I wasn't aware of my brokenness. I was a broken cistern.

"For My people have committed two evils:
They have abandoned (rejected) Me,
The fountain of living water,
And they have carved out their own cisterns,
Broken cisterns
That cannot hold water." Jeremiah 2:13 (AMP)

I found myself exhausted all the time trying to please people, especially my mother. My husband said I would turn into a different person when she was around or after I hung up the phone from speaking with her. I was awful. She not only made me feel terrible, but her toxic behavior morphed me into a distasteful person towards others, towards those closest to me, the ones I love. I remember Walt repeatedly saying, "Hurting people, hurt people." I didn't understand what he meant and was too prideful to ask. Later I learned what my husband intended to say. Hurting people, who have been mistreated or wounded either verbally or physically (which affects our emotional, mental, and spiritual health), will most likely hurt others. Unfortunately, abused people are usually incapable of recognizing doing so. Whenever this occurred, He would ask me why I would allow my mother to hurt me. I didn't have an answer. I didn't know how to respond to him or have any special skills to keep her from harming me. I tried not to let her get under my skin, but my efforts were worthless. After twenty-five years of getting beaten down mentally and emotionally, I just couldn't do it by myself. No matter what I said or did was ever going to be good enough for my mother's acceptance. I was broken. I felt abandoned, useless, and unworthy. Little did I know Jesus was watching. Jesus saw everything I went through. He knew my heart was broken, and my mind was in a state of confusion because He knows all of our thoughts.

> "For the Lord searches all hearts and minds and understands all the wanderings of the thoughts…" 1 Chronicles 28:9 (AMPC)

> "For the Lord sees not as man sees; for man looks on the outward appearance, but the Lord looks on the heart." 1 Samuel 16:7 (AMPC)

> "But O Lord of hosts, Who judges rightly and justly, Who tests the heart and the mind,…" Jeremiah 11:20 (AMPC)

During those early years of marriage, little did I know the Lord was revealing Himself to me, little by little, through small things—life's simple pleasures. Although I wanted to honor the Lord by honoring or, in my case, pleasing my mother, it seemed like Jesus was starting to grab my attention. For instance, I started focusing on Him more as I noticed Him blessing me with little desires of my heart. The result was it took my attention away from trying to please my mother. His truth, His love for me, and His delight in me grabbed my attention. I no longer focused on my mother's approval and instead was grateful for Jesus' blessings. He was meeting my needs. He gave me favor with my boss at work, and He provided me with a good used washer and dryer soon after moving into our home and a set of bunk beds for the boys, just at the perfect time.

One of my most memorable blessings was how we obtained money for our Volvo, an accident in disguise. One day, when we were traveling with our little family in our car, I had moved from sitting in the passenger's seat to the back seat to take care of the boys when suddenly we were hit. Without notice, the driver hit our car on the driver's side, allowing Walt room to shift to the passenger side of our vehicle quickly. My merciful husband, showing loving-kindness to the elderly lady who hit us, calmed her fears. She was so grateful that no one was hurt; she blessed us with enough money to compensate for damages to our vehicle. In turn, the accident made it possible to buy our much-needed second vehicle, our safe Volvo. Was this coincidence or providence? I started to notice how God graciously and lovingly bestowed little miracles upon us. I saw His hand orchestrating our lives. The manifestation of my secret prayers were being fulfilled. And my heart became more and more grateful for all of them.

I was increasingly aware and in awe of Jesus' Spirit of Truth and His love for me as I reflected on His goodness. However, I also became confused as fear tried to find a home in my heart and mind. My heart carried many scars and was vulnerable from numerous traumas I experienced during my childhood years. Like many, I experienced sexual abuse as a child, which left me feeling dirty, disobedient, alone, abandoned, and shameful. When I finally felt courageous enough to tell my parents, they accused me of lying. I thought my parents would protect me. The injustice was evidence of a disobedient lifestyle. A lifestyle that follows the dictates of the flesh and not the Spirit. I couldn't understand how my parents, some extended family members, and others I've witnessed could have been leaders of churches or Christian organizations when peace or true fellowship rarely existed in our homes. I saw them act one way in public, but at home or not within public view, I experienced a spirit of contention—gossiping, backbiting, and criticizing. Unfortunately, more days of negative behaviors not being dealt with escalated to adultery, physical abuse, then ultimately, divorces.

I was earnestly determined not to repeat the same pattern with my young family. No way, not on my watch! So, I started to pray more, not knowing exactly how He would heal the brokenness, but God saw everything, knew my heart, and was faithful to His promises. He heard the questions I asked in my mind and listened to my prayers while watching. Even though I felt God was not answering rapidly enough, He was behind the scenes working on my behalf the whole time and is still working!

The consequences of disobedience (sin) are inevitable. The apostle Paul spoke to believers, emphasizing that we must no longer live like heathens. He stated, "Their moral understanding is darkened, and their reasoning is beclouded. [They are] alienated (estranged, self-banished) from the life of God [with no share in it; this is] because of the ignorance (the want of knowledge and perception, the willful blindness) that is deep seated in them, due to their hardness of heart [to the insensitiveness of their moral nature]." Ephesians 4:18 (AMPC)

> The Word of the Lord says in Hosea 4:6 (AMP),
> "My people are destroyed for lack of knowledge
> [of My law, where I reveal My will];"

> And in Isaiah 5:13 (AMP), "Therefore My people
> go into exile because they lack knowledge [of God];
> And their honorable men are famished, And their
> common people are parched with thirst."

My genuine desire was for Walt and me to form a loving home without strife or malice. I wanted a home of peace—a place where family members would lift each other up rather than tearing each other down. The words of Isaiah, "And their honorable men are famished" stood out to me. I was hungry for righteous living and wanted to experience blessings of peace. To do that, I would have needed a harmonious example of family life and a thorough knowledge of God's Word—good discipleship. At that point, I had neither and was in bondage without realizing it. I failed to recognize the hardness in my heart that had occurred as a child developing from a family life that was dysfunctional and inconsistent with God's word.

Some of the dysfunctionality came from an inadequate relationship with my parents. The desire for desperately wanting a mother-daughter relationship went deep. Approximately seven years after Walt and I were married was when the Lord revealed the hidden sorrows I had experienced as a child. The deep-seated deprivation contributed to my brokenness and the reason behind my hardened heart. I later realized I was trying to fulfill a void of love.

I wasn't content with just having our two boys. Something was missing. I loved my husband and our family, but I sensed it wasn't complete. I purposed to have a third child in my heart, and I begged the Lord for a girl, a daughter to call my own. I yearned to experience a mother and daughter's unique love and relationship, to be loved unconditionally and to love. I desired to teach and encourage my daughter in a way that I could never experience during my life as a child and young adult. I wanted to delight in her and enjoy her, just because she's mine. There were so many things I wanted to share with her that I knew I wouldn't be able to impart with our sons. A mother-son relationship is not quite the same. I prayed and held on to God's word, "Lord, your word says that if I delight myself in You, You will give me the desires of my heart." Psalm 37:4 (NKJV).

During the months of my third pregnancy, in the late summer of 1995, my husband Walt had a dream. One morning he woke up and said to me, "I had a dream we had a baby girl! I was carrying her in our office in a car seat, an infant car seat." I asked Walt, what she looked like, and he said, "She had dark brown hair and light skin, chunky (like all our babies), but I couldn't see her face. I knew it was a girl because she was all dolled up, with a ribbon in her hair, as you would dress her."

This prophecy was from one of the first dreams Walt shared with me that he had received from the Lord. From then on, Walt usually shares his dreams with me. I have learned to pay close attention and heed or ponder and ask the Lord for discernment when He speaks through Walt. Peter reminds us of scripture spoken from the prophet Joel (2:28) that God's Spirit is with us through different revelations:

"'AND IT SHALL BE IN THE LAST DAYS,' SAYS GOD,
'THAT I WILL POUR OUT MY SPIRIT UPON ALL MANKIND;
AND YOUR SONS AND YOUR DAUGHTERS SHALL PROPHESY,
AND YOUR YOUNG MEN SHALL SEE
[DIVINELY PROMPTED] VISIONS,
AND YOUR OLD MEN SHALL DREAM [DIVINELY
PROMPTED] DREAMS;" Acts 2:17 (AMP)

Prophecies are both blessings and warnings. They can be good news or a wake-up call, a warning. Nonetheless, because we serve, believe, and trust in a great God who creates all things and knows all things, from beginning to end, we should never fear or feel afraid. He is the same yesterday, today, and tomorrow.

"Jesus Christ is [eternally changeless, always] the same
yesterday and today and forever." Hebrews 13:8 (AMP)

When we choose to listen and see with our spiritual ears and eyes (because God is Spirit), we can know Him, His plans for our lives, our future.

"For I know the plans and thoughts that I have
for you,' says the Lord, 'plans for peace and well-
being and not for disaster, to give you a future and a
hope. Then you will call on Me and you will come

and pray to Me, and I will hear [your voice] and I
will listen to you." Jeremiah 29:11–12 (AMP)

Walt and I were extremely excited. I thought to myself, *Could this be true?* I remember the moment like it was yesterday. We were in our bedroom, living in a small nine-hundred-square-foot house in Alhambra, California. Just as Mary, the mother of Jesus, pondered in her heart when the shepherds shared the good news of Jesus' birth, I pondered too. I asked myself, *Could God love me so much as to give me the desire of my heart?* I really wanted to believe our new baby was indeed a girl during that moment. *Could God do it? I knew He could, of course, He could. Would He do it? I believed He would.* The real question was, *Why?* It was not due to anything I had done or who I was. That's for sure. My mother told me my entire life that I was lazy like my father. Growing up, I was hardly given encouragement or positive affirmation. None of my accomplishments were considered good enough; at least those were my mother's opinions. So in my heart and mind, I believed the dream Walt shared with me of having a little girl, hoping it would come true.

This experience wasn't the first time God spoke to me. It was the first time He spoke through Walt, and there has been several encounters throughout our thirty-two years of marriage. But before this event, little did I know it was God encouraging me—loving me which was building up my faith in Him. He was taking the broken pieces of my life and making them whole. That's what He does if you let Him. It was the beginning stages of the restoration I had prayed about. My faith was strengthening as I learned to trust, wait, and continue believing while He was transforming me.

My first encounter was when I was sixteen years old, as far back as I can remember. I had a dream, a vision, of having a little boy. He was about four or five years old, dark hair, a clean-cut little boy. I was taking him to school in a dark green SUV-type vehicle. The school was an older traditional building with steps leading to the front office, positioned at the front of the school. I saw him on the steps with his backpack as I held his little hand, leading him inside; that is when my dream suddenly stopped. Quickly waking up, I thought to myself, *That's a crazy dream, and what is its significance?* Fast forward to 1995, and it hit me! I recalled my dream when I took our first son, Jared, to school in Alhambra! His first day of school was the fulfillment of the vision I experienced many years prior! We didn't own a green SUV during the time, but we did have one when Jared was a baby. Once I stood in front of the school, which I found familiar, I knew I had been there before. During that moment, the Holy Spirit reminded me of the vision I had when I was sixteen years old. Coincidence? Or providence?

Experiencing encounters with Jesus and His Holy Spirit, I have become familiar with His voice and promises, when I read His Word.

> Jesus said, "My sheep hear My voice, and
> I know them, and they follow Me."
> John 10:27 (NKJV)

It wasn't that I didn't trust the Lord upon hearing Walt's dream of carrying a baby girl. It was the notion of not deserving to be blessed or loved enough to be given such a great gift, a desire I longed for.

Four
To Know Him

That I may know him, and the power of his
resurrection, and the fellowship of his sufferings,
being made conformable unto his death;
—Philippians 3:10 (KJV)

God is true to His word. In Numbers 23:19 (NKJV), God declares to Balak, "God is not a man, that He should lie, Nor a son of man, that He should repent. Has He said, and will He not do?" When we pray, believing He will hear and answer our prayers, He will do it. He will answer. They may not happen in our timing or how we may anticipate. God loves us so much and knows what's best for us; sometimes, the answer may be "no." Similar to a parent knowing more than their child, He knows more.

"For my thoughts are not your thoughts, neither are your
ways my ways, saith the Lord. For as the heavens are higher
than the earth, so are my ways higher than your ways, and
my thoughts than your thoughts." Isaiah 55:8–9 (KJV)

Either way, He answers. God is sovereign and, like a parent who loves their child, will do what's best for that child.

In December 1995, I took off the day from work to spend our entire anniversary day celebrating our new baby. My husband and I had planned an anniversary breakfast together before going to the doctor's office. We had an early appointment to have an ultrasound to confirm the health and sex of our new baby girl. Afterward, we would finish spending the day together. Unfortunately, the day did not play out that way. I don't recall having breakfast at all, and the staff postponed our morning doctor's appointment until the end of the day. We waited more than six hours to see the doctor and have the ultrasound done. I took the day off from work, our boys were taken care of at home, and I was determined to find out if the baby I was carrying was indeed a girl. Finally, about 6 p.m., the nurses called us into the examining room. As I was lying on the table while the doctor was administering the ultrasound, before she said anything, I realized. I noticed an image I was familiar with during my last two pregnancies. The tears started to roll from my eyes as my heart sank like a heavy anchor moving quickly to the bottom of the ocean. It seemed like a flood came over me. My loving husband looked at me, concerned. He couldn't fix it. The doctor was pleased to announce that the baby boy was healthy, giving us the due date and other pertinent information. All I could think of was the vision Walt had, his dream. Quickly, my mind switched directions. Instead of being crushed over not having a girl, I immediately began thanking the Lord for the beautiful, healthy baby boy He chose to give us instead. I didn't fully understand why He would provide us with that dream of having a baby girl, but I decided to be grateful.

In the Spring of 1996, after giving birth to our third son, Tyler, I heeded the call of full-time-motherhood, quit my position at the microfilm company, and stayed home. It was a new season for Walt and me, as he focused on his career and worked more hours while I was caring for our boys. The decision to quit my job was difficult because I loved helping people and enjoyed my job and the company I worked for. However, during the last six months of my pregnancy with Tyler, I felt the Lord calling me to stay home. Those drives to work while listening to the radio had prepared me to say "yes" to becoming a stay-at-home mom. I felt compelled to let go of what I was familiar with, working with adults in an office environment, to become the person God was calling me to be for this new season of my life.

Although I loved the concept of marriage and family, I didn't quite know how to build it or develop it in a healthy manner. My childhood experiences and role models were not optimal, and I wanted an improved, peaceful, loving family without the drama. Well, when you have children, there's drama, but how you handle or respond to the drama could make a difference in having peace in the home. Little did I know that it would take plenty of changes in me to accomplish this. I found myself busy doing mommy and wifey things during the daytime. Yet after the boys were asleep, it was too quiet. I was home alone with the children, all day and all night. Walt worked his career in the real estate industry during the day while working graveyard shifts at restaurants to keep food on our table and a roof over our heads.

I stayed up late watching Christian television programs many nights, which led me to read my Bible and study it. Previously, I opened my Bible when I attended church and studied Religion in college. I kept hearing sermons on being an overcomer and living on the promises of God. I wanted to know more about how to accomplish these goals. So, I started from the beginning, the book of Genesis. The more I read, the more familiar Sunday School lessons replayed in my mind. During this young adult season in my life, I was paying closer attention as I read the stories in my Bible.

This time I took copious notes and literally wrote my prayers and revelations in the margins of my Bible pages. The more I read, the more I fell in love with Jesus.

I didn't understand the entirety of what I read, but I felt near to Him. I learned about the animal sacrifices and how certain animals had to be perfect to present to the Lord continuously for the remission of sins of the Jewish people. It amazed and humbled me. I compared those offerings to the ultimate sacrifice Christ bestowed upon us at the cross and marveled at the symbolic references that spoke of the prophecies of His messianic coming. Again, I didn't understand all that I read, but the very basics humbled me. I found myself kneeling and sobbing in gratitude for what He did for me, my husband, our children, and the world. I wanted to know Him and the power of His resurrection. I desired to be an overcomer like Jesus was when He walked on earth. I resolved to have my marriage close and strong. I aspired my children to know Him, not only as Savior, but Lord of their lives. I wanted my family, our children, to follow Him and not experience similar hypocrisy, which cultivated the dysfunction in a home I experienced as a child. I wanted to be like Jesus and partake in the power of overcoming and show them how to love and be loved. I was resolute in knowing Jesus as referenced here:

"Yes, furthermore, I count everything as loss compared to the possession of the priceless privilege (the overwhelming preciousness, the surpassing worth, and supreme advantage) of knowing Christ Jesus my Lord and of progressively becoming more deeply and intimately acquainted with Him [of perceiving and recognizing and understanding Him more fully and clearly]. For His sake I have lost everything and consider it all to be mere rubbish (refuse, dregs), in order that I may win (gain) Christ (the Anointed One). And that I may [actually] be found and know as in Him, not having any [self-achieved] righteousness that can be called my own, based on my obedience to the Law's demands (ritualistic uprightness and supposed right standing with God thus acquired), but possessing that [genuine righteousness] which comes through faith in Christ (Anointed One), the [truly] right standing with God, which comes from God by [saving] faith. [For my determined purpose is] that I may know Him [that I may progressively become more deeply and intimately acquainted with Him, perceiving and recognizing and understanding the wonders of His person more strongly and more clearly], and that I may in that same way come to know the power outflowing from His resurrection [which it exerts over believers], and that I may so share His sufferings as to be continually transformed [in Spirit into His likeness even] to His death, [in the hope] That if possible I may attain to the [spiritual and moral] resurrection [that lifts me] out from among the dead [even while in the body]. Not that I have now attained [this ideal], or have already been made perfect, but I press on to lay hold of (grasp) and make my own, that for which Christ Jesus (the Messiah) has laid hold of me and made me His own." Philippians 3:8–11 (AMPC)

Little did I know my spiritual desire to know Christ Jesus better would take me on a very challenging journey. It was a journey of whittling away at the bad habits I had developed during my upbringing. He was peeling off selfishness like an onion (although I didn't think I was selfish). I now realize what my past behavior was like. He was also peeling off insecurity and the conduct of such cultivation. The frequent criticism had rooted adverse decisions as I matured. After repenting, I started memorizing the wonderful, uplifting, encouraging promises in His Word. I was tenacious. Today, I am still determined to know Him more and the power of the resurrection, even if it means sharing in His sufferings. Yes, this is what it means, what it takes to KNOW HIM! But I thank God for His endless mercy and love, loving-kindness, and insurmountable grace. Little did I know that everything I was going to go through was in His hands.

During the last few months at my job and before the birth of our third son, Tyler, Walt noticed how skilled and diligent I was at my work. I would bring work home to complete for the next day when I had to. When one of the department managers would make mistakes on the employee's paychecks, I would have payroll make the corrections and overnight the employees' paychecks for them to receive on Saturday morning, rather than having the workers wait until Monday. My work ethic encouraged my husband to suggest I study and obtain my real estate license. He said I would be well suited for real estate because of my diligence in ensuring the employees were adequately cared for. So, I took his advice and prepared for my real estate exam soon after Tyler was born. My husband saw something in me, which I couldn't see in myself. He saw a competent, tenacious person who enjoyed helping other people. It was baffling to believe him due to multiple years of negativity and lies directed towards me while growing up. But, by faith, I took a chance to walk in the belief my loving husband had for me. It seemed as though Jesus was demonstrating His love for me through Walt. My mind was beginning to be renewed by devotedly reading God's word, trusting Him, and taking steps in the opposite direction from my upbringing. At first, believing my husband felt very foreign to me. Still, with his unvarying encouragement and love, I began feeling confident with my renewed trust in God.

Tyler was about six months old when I prepared to take my real estate license exam. Before my exam date, I took a weekend crash course for a deep study to ensure my knowledge of real estate law, vocabulary, finance, etc. That weekend was when I met Desion. Desion was wearing a t-shirt with a big yellow smiling face with the words "I love Jesus" on it. I'm a little leery of people who wear big flashy "I love Jesus" clothes or place Christian bumper stickers on their cars. For some reason, when I saw things like these, the first word that came to mind was *hypocrisy*. So, I was inclined to stay away from people like them. But now, I'm not worried about the hypocrisy because I quickly realized not one person on this earth is perfect, except Jesus. I am guilty as charged. We are all a mess! So instead of pre-judging them, I now approach them and ask questions, like, "Tell me, why do you love Jesus?" Asking questions allows me to edify and share the goodness of Jesus with them and fellowship with them. And if they're hurting, it presents an opportunity to pray with and for them. It's all about glorifying the name of Jesus!

So, as I prepared to get in my car to get lunch, Desion approached me and asked if I wanted to drive and have lunch with her and another gal who was also taking the crash course. I agreed, so after arriving at the fast-food restaurant, I sat down at the table while she ordered her food. Strangely, she turned and peculiarly looked at me. Desion was wearing sunglasses, but she pulled them down slightly off her face to get a better look at me. I thought to myself, *What's going on? Was the counter food-server asking her a question about my food?* When she completed her order and paid for her food, she approached the table where I was sitting.

I later discovered that Desion heard a word from the Lord to give me. Since the Lord knew I didn't trust her, He had given her the color of my kitchen window curtains and other details from my thoughts only God knew. During our quick lunch, she shared with me some unbelievable details of my life. Details in my heart I was struggling with that only God knew. What the Lord had given Desion was so on target and full of encouragement, I was overcome with joy! As we walked to our cars at the restaurant parking lot, a spirit of laughter came over me. It was so heavy, so dense I couldn't stop! It was the Joy of the Lord! It was so full of unspeakable happiness, like the weight of the world was lifted off my shoulders. Looking back, I don't recall all the details from the real estate course that weekend, other than asking the Lord for help. I said, "Lord, I believe everyone should have the opportunity to own their own home, to have a place to call their own. If this is what you want for my life, please help me pass this exam." Sure enough, I passed and have been helping people live the American dream of owning their homes or commercial buildings since then.

Desion and I kept in touch for a while after that weekend. A couple of years later, she had invited me to attend her baby shower. As I was near the street, walking towards the front door of her house, Desion stood at the front door, looking strangely at me. Concerned, I said, "What?" referring to the clothes I was wearing while looking down and around myself. She said, "I see a little girl behind you peeking her head out." "What?" I replied. Once again, she said, "Yeah! A little girl is hiding behind you, holding onto your legs!" I replied, "You're being ridiculous." Then I went inside the house and never thought about it again.

Tyler was about two years old when I noticed the age differences between him and his elder brothers. There were five members in our family, and I didn't want Tyler to feel left out. For some reason, I felt our family was incomplete, so I reasoned to have another child; unknowingly, I was already pregnant. Upon finding out I was pregnant, I was a little frightened because Walt was pretty stressed when first hearing about me carrying Tyler. Two boys were a busy handful, but another boy? What were the odds of having a girl? I think that's why the Lord had given Walt the vision of the baby girl. Maybe he needed some reassurance or some hope. The fear of telling my husband I was pregnant for the fourth time lasted until I couldn't hide it from him any longer. Walt is a very hard worker. I didn't know how to break it to him. Somehow, I felt like I was letting him down. It was near the beginning of my second trimester, about five months pregnant when I gave Walt the news. It was also the time when we could find out what the sex of the baby was. Because of our previous experience and my willingness to accept whatever God gave us, I had no desire to know the sex of the baby. None whatsoever. So, after I had my ultrasound, my sneaky husband called the doctor to find out the sex of our new baby and tried to convince me that I wanted to know. I remember sitting on our living room chair while he knelt, begging to share the news with me. Right then, I knew it was a girl. My husband is the worst at keeping surprises from me. When he's excited about giving me a gift, he has no reservations about surprising me with it or even wrapping it. He just gives it. That man went all out for Teagan's baby shower. I was very appreciative, but I was cautious not to excite myself beforehand and wait until after the baby was born to confirm it was a girl.

I was in such denial of God's providence. When I was about eight months pregnant, after taking the older boys to school and while Tyler took his nap, I took a much-needed shower and had a prayerful moment. I concluded praying over the boys and Walt when the Holy Spirit said to me, "What about that one?" Meaning the one in my womb. Immediately I thought, *I'm so sorry Lord, I forgot!* So, I placed my hand over my belly and prayed for the baby. Something came over me. I was travailing or praying in the Spirit heavily. When I finished my shower, I started to feel a little hope. I just really wanted a healthy baby and a safe delivery. I had surrendered my desire of having a baby girl and wanted whatever the Lord wanted to grant me.

In the afternoon of September 20, 1998, I was resting on my bed reading, while the boys were playing, when I started feeling contractions. By this time, I was a professional child-bearer. So, I just lied on my bed and waited until the contractions felt stronger and closer together. I called Walt to tell him what was happening, and he said, "I'm coming now to take you to the hospital." We ended up arguing over the phone because I wasn't ready yet, but then he said, "Honey, your deliveries come quickly, and I want to make sure you're ok." After Walt and I hung up, I called my sisters and mom to watch over the boys. A few hours later, there she was—a beautiful, healthy baby girl whom her daddy and I finally named Teagan. I had the privilege of calling our boys, but I just couldn't find a suitable name for our daughter. It wasn't until mine and Teagan's final evening at the hospital when Walt called, mentioning some names and their meanings he liked, to share with me. We decided on *Teagan* for her first name, which means "beautiful baby girl" in Welsh. I figured this was our last child and only girl, so there wouldn't be any sibling conflict. We chose *Rylee* for her middle name, Irish for "courageous or valiant." Then our surname is *Wehrmann*, German for "warrior, soldier, defender." When Walt and I settled on her name, little did we know she would live up to those characters: Beautiful – Courageous – Warrior.

As I held the desire-of-my-heart in my arms, gazing at her beautiful, lush, dark brown hair and eyes, her chunky, precious cheeks and legs, I was so amazed at how God kept His word. Our beautiful miracle. He delivered on His promise to us. Not when we thought, because he had to perform some physical plumbing arrangements with my hormones, but He came through. Now I'm convinced of His faithfulness. His fierce love for me.

Five
The Cup

♡

Let be and be still, and know (recognize and understand)
that I am God. I will be exalted among the nations! I
will be exalted in the earth! The Lord of hosts is with
us; the God of Jacob is our Refuge (our High Tower and
Stronghold). Selah [pause, and calmly think of that]!
—Psalm 46:10–11 (AMPC)

T hat Wednesday afternoon was one of the longest and hardest
days Walt and I have ever experienced in our marriage, in
our lives. It was February 15, 2017, and our baby girl was lying in
a hospital bed fighting for her life. Or was she? I have never felt so
helpless in my life. I could not protect her. As Walt and I were in
Teagan's hospital room, the surgical doctors came to see if there
was any movement from Teagan after performing the second brain
surgery. They informed us that they were monitoring her closely for
any brain activity response.

I attended a woman's Bible study group at a local church during
this season. When I was more informed on how to pray for Teagan,
I immediately texted a couple of the group's leaders to send out a

prayer alert, asking them to pray specifically for Teagan's brain. I couldn't remember the medical terms the doctor had given us, but I did my best to explain to the ladies what we were all hoping for, which was the complete healing of her brain. I didn't even think to have them pray God's will over Teagan's life, not even for her vital organs that were crushed and barely functioning. My mind was in such disarray that I didn't know how to pray. It seemed like I was rushing and blurting out words without remembering what I had just said. Usually, my prayers are strategic by praying His Word over the situation and speaking or confessing His promises. I presented my heart humbly, yet courageously, before His throne of mercy and grace. But not this time. I searched for scripture to read, confess, and declare as I had my Bible open. I couldn't find anything! I tried this many times through the several days we spent in her hospital room. There was nothing. Silence filled the atmosphere. I knew God was with us as I felt His love, although it seemed He had abandoned us. I was in a state of confusion. Nonetheless, I knew my heavenly Father was closely listening to and watching everything. I held on to my experiences with Him, His faithfulness.

Walt and I were hungry and extremely tired. When Tyler arrived at the hospital, he was outraged and wanted revenge. I had to calm his emotions. I sensed he was angry that someone hurt his baby sister and fearful of understanding her condition. Since only two of Teagan's brothers, Zach and Tyler, were with us at the hospital, Jared, her eldest brother, was the last family member who was absent. The hospital staff told us that they would send out a message to Red Cross. The Red Cross would then deliver the message to Jared's unit officer, telling him the circumstances and the urgency to come home immediately. Jared flew to the states and was home with us by that Friday.

While the hospital was keeping a close eye on Teagan, there was nothing more we could do. So my husband and I decided to get some food to eat, change our clothes, and gird ourselves for the worst possible news. Leaving Teagan's hospital bed, we went downstairs. As we approached the lobby, we noticed a small group of people waiting for us. They seemed hesitant to meet us, so I went to them and told them who Walt and I were. Surprisingly, they said, "We know. We've been waiting for you." and started introducing themselves. The first person was Anthony's mom, Danielle.

Immediately, my heart went out to her with grief and compassion as I asked her how Anthony was doing. She shared with us that he was under observation and explained some of his injuries. Still, overall the doctors thought he would be well enough to go home the next day or Friday. I was so relieved to hear Anthony was physically going to be ok. I told Danielle how sorry I was. I was remorseful for the whole thing and what they had to go through. But I was glad to hear that she would be able to have her son back again. While I was saying this, I thought of our daughter's death weighing in the balance. We desperately hoped Teagan would be whole again. Better than whole, supernaturally renewed for God's glory. That was my desire.

Before leaving the hospital, the chaplain drew near to us very cautiously. I sensed she didn't want to disturb us, yet hesitantly needed to tell us, me, something. As I looked at her countenance, it was as though she was thinking (or listening to the Lord) of what or how to say what she needed to say. Then she spoke. With bold confidence, her soft tone spoke words cautiously, "Be still and know I AM God." Instantly, my thoughts were screaming, *WHAT? What does this mean?* I'm sure the look on my face was that of frustration mixed with perplexity as well as exhaustion and who knows what else. I was spent from crying, so I tried to hold in my tears and accepted her words. Besides, I knew it wasn't her speaking to me, it was the Lord through her. Here I was, pondering again, with so many questions in my head and wondering what this word meant for our family, or was it just for me?

After eating and going home to change, we returned to the hospital to spend the night with Teagan. It was our routine for now. Every moment we spent with her, we would talk to her and tell her we loved her. I would pace her room while looking for Bible scripture to speak life into her and declare God's Word over her, but there was no sign of response from her. Although God's presence, the love I felt in my spirit, was so heavily upon me, yet I did not hear any direction from Him. I could not hear His voice. I still felt abandoned, although persistently expecting Him to show up. I was waiting for Him to perform His miracle in her. I wasn't giving up.

I was drained in every capacity and needed to be filled. I needed to be surrounded by God's people and hear His Word. So the next day, Thursday, I went to my women's Bible study. Arriving to sit amongst the women, I noticed an unusual number of ladies at our table and in our group. I didn't recognize some of them, but it didn't matter to me because I focused on wanting spiritual substance. I needed to hear from my Heavenly Father. Seemingly, I had taken the women by surprise. They must have thought I should have been at the hospital. They didn't say much, but I felt all eyes were upon me. There were some goodies in the middle of the table and one purple (my favorite color) coffee mug left that no one had taken. The cups were little gifts given to the women that day, which was unconventional. I asked the ladies at my table if the coffee cup belonged to anyone, and they replied, "No." and motioned for me to take it.

As I picked up the cup, I peered at the scripture verse written on it. To my surprise, it said, "Be still and know that I Am God. Psalms 46:10!" (ASV) Immediately I knew God never abandoned me. Coincidence? Or providence? He knew I needed Him more than ever, and the cup was a reminder of His sovereign power in this whole situation. There was nothing I could say, do or think! Nothing! He is God, and He was in control over it all. All I needed to do was to be still and rest in Him. Trust Him and see Him work. To surrender my will and see Him glorify and reveal Himself to me and the world around me. I'm so grateful that cup was left for me. I believe He arranged it just for me at the perfect place and perfect time. He knew this tenacious daughter of His would not relent in search of an answer. His cup given to me was a confirmation of His Word through the chaplain and a constant reminder as I daily have my morning coffee with Him that He is the great I AM!

Jesus—Jehovah—God—YHWH (YAHWEH)—I AM!

Exodus 3:14 –15 (AMPC) reads, "I AM WHO I AM and WHAT I AM, and I WILL BE WHAT I WILL BE. This is My name forever, and by this name, I am to be remembered to all generations." (paraphrased)

I heard a pastor once say, "God's character is not defined by our notions of what He ought to be (I wanted God to be Jehovah-Rophe, The LORD who heals—physically speaking), but by what He chooses to reveal about Himself!"

- "God's name is His self-revelation."—Charles Ellicott, A Bible Commentary.
- "The name signifies the active presence of the person in the fullness of the revealed character."—J.D. Douglas et al. eds., The New Bible Dictionary.

He revealed LOVE to Me. God *IS* Love. Jehovah was and is FIERCELY LOVE!! Unfathomable, impenetrable, uncontainable, unmeasurable, LOVE! I can go on, but my words cannot explain, nor my mind understand to adequately measure the depth of Him through this fleeting body of mine.

Little did I know there were quite a few women at my table who had each lost a child. I learned of this several weeks later as time went on. Still, while Teagan was lying in the hospital bed during that solemn week, some of those women gravitated towards me. It was the wonder of Jesus they saw in me as His love overflowed from me to mend the sorrow in their hearts. I sensed they needed to see what a person with hope looks like, as they, themselves, longed to be filled with hope—the kind of hope that only God can mend and anchor from a broken heart. No religion or psychological therapy can remedy such a tragedy! We can only find this hope in the one and only Living God who fiercely loves us! A God who desperately wants us restored from this sinful world's deathly antics to Himself! His unfailing love! To overcome and live life abundantly!

> "The thief comes only in order to steal and kill and destroy. I came that they may have and enjoy life, and have it in abundance (to the full, till it overflows)."
> John 10:10 (AMPC)

No amount of education or money can uphold the power of God. No matter how rich or poor, educated or not—none of those things matter to Him. The only thing that matters is if we believe. It's the condition of our hearts when we trust and rely on His sovereign power. Only Jesus can save us!

So I concluded that it was my sold-out-for-Jesus boldness, expressed by His unfathomable fierce love, that drew people to me. They wanted to know my secret. I recall having conversations with people who had gone through losses years ago. Something triggered them to remember certain things that would then make them sob— they could still feel the sting of death. As they shared, the Holy Spirit would give me a word to share hope with them. I could immediately see the change in their countenance from being in darkness to light, from sorrow to joy, hopelessness to full of hope. Thus, having experienced an everlasting revelation gave them so much hope and understanding, as God would instantly heal their hearts, minds, and emotions. Only Jehovah God, the great I AM, can do this. Only Jesus Christ our Lord and Savior. The hope of the world.

> "This hope [this confident assurance] we have as an anchor of the soul [it cannot slip and it cannot break down under whatever pressure bears upon it]—a safe and steadfast hope that enters within the veil [of the heavenly temple, that most Holy Place in which the very presence of God dwells]," Hebrews 6:19 (AMP)

Thursday afternoon, on February 16, 2017, Walt and I received the news we didn't want to hear nor accept. The doctors told us that Teagan's brain was not responding, and they pronounced her dead that day. I refused to believe those words. Keeping my composure, I nodded my head to the doctors with disbelief in my heart and mind. They told us that we needed to get used to the new normal. I vehemently hated those words! We responded and told the medical staff that our son, Jared, was on his way home from his deployment in Turkey. We asked if the hospital and staff would give us some time with her until her big brother arrived to say goodbye. The doctors and hospital staff agreed, so we continued to pray and believe. Besides, if Lazarus was in his tomb for over three days and Jesus raised him from the dead, why couldn't Jesus raise Teagan from her bed?

I'm not sure if it was on Thursday or Friday, but Anthony, Teagan's friend who was in the car with her at the time of the accident, was released from the hospital. Before leaving, he asked us for permission to see Teagan one last time and to have a private moment with her. We said, "Yes, of course." That poor kid was so broken up over her; there wasn't anything I could say or do to comfort him. I think he really cared for her. I just hugged him, and he left. I've prayed for Anthony and his family that God would heal and restore each of them the only way God knows how. They're a wonderful family who accepted and cared for Teagan like their own. I appreciated them showing love towards her and giving her a sense of family. It was what Teagan missed when her brothers had left home. She missed our big family. When Teagan was with Anthony, I knew his family filled the loneliness of not having her brothers present.

It was Friday when Jared visited his sister Teagan. Although, the hospital didn't know which brother he was until after the weekend. Walt and I took the opportunity of having additional days with Teagan to continue praying and walking, walking and praying, believing our miracle could come. I extended my prayer walk area to the whole floor. I would walk up and down the hallway, looking at and praying for the other patients, praying for their salvation and healing. Walt and I left the hospital only once during each day to eat, shower, and change our clothes. Then we returned to spend nights beside Teagan on a narrow bay-window bench, sleeping head to toe, if we even slept at all.

Saturday came, and it felt like a zoo in the ICU ward. Some people from church came to pray; my two younger sisters with some of their family members had arrived, my mother was there, and of course, our three sons were present that morning as well. My youngest sister sought attention by telling stories and engaging in conversations in an effort to make the heaviness and anxiety dissipate. I'm sure she meant well, but this event didn't belong to her, although tension seemed to subside a bit. After the church people felt their efforts were complete, there was a beautiful moment when my sisters and I sang over Teagan. We just sang to Jesus, praising Him for her. Soon afterward, our sons requested individual time alone with Teagan to say goodbye. Walt and I respected their request and had everyone wait outside the ICU ward, at the lobby near the elevators.

The girls—meaning my mother, sisters, niece, and myself—gathered together, while Walt and Teagan's brothers, along with their uncles, gathered in a separate group in the same area. While the girls huddled together, my niece gave me a picture that she drew for Teagan. As I went to hug Sarah to thank her, a profound sadness came over me. I found myself letting out an agonizing wail—knowing I would never get to hold my daughter again. I felt such an intense pain while crying out; at the same time, I knew in my spirit I was letting Teagan go. I knew in my heart that the Lord planned to keep her with Him. As I held on tight to my niece, it felt bittersweet, as if I was holding Teagan for the last time. Quickly, I gained my composure and apologized to my niece and sister, hoping I had not hurt them somehow. Walt, my loving husband, recognized my deep pain and came beside me to console me.

In my anguish, I quickly remembered Jesus' last cry in Matthew 27:50 (AMPC), "And Jesus cried again with a loud voice and gave up His spirit."

My distress could not compare to Jesus' suffering as He died at the cross. Still, just a smidge of the sting of death He experienced, I experienced. Was this coincidence or providence? I was participating in His sufferings. It was final. The great I AM gave me His answer to our prayer. It was, "No." And that was that. When Walt and I both realized Teagan wouldn't be coming back to us, Walt said, "You know, I think the Lord had given a choice to Teagan whether to stay with Him or return to us, and she chose to stay with Him." I agreed with Walt's reasoning. Seriously, who in heaven, experiencing such great LOVE, would want to come back to this mad world when the alternative was paradise? That's a no-brainer. That's why I felt sorry for Lazarus. You know, the story in the Bible of the friend Jesus raised from the dead? The poor guy left paradise and came back to live in this sinful, painful, yet wonderful world for quite some time afterward.

Now I understand why my mother exclaimed, "Like Job!" the first day when we were sitting in the little room, with the little window, which had panes shaped like a cross. The Lord was trying to tell me something. I guess I was like Job, in the sense that I did not charge God foolishly for taking Teagan. I did not blame Him, nor was I bitter. I never said or thought a negative word toward my loving Heavenly Father. I just stood still. And in that stillness, I worshiped Him. I surrendered my will. Job's account in chapter 1 verses 20–22 (AMP) states this:

> "Then Job got up and tore his robe and shaved his
> head [in mourning for the children], and he fell
> to the ground and worshiped [God]. He said,
> "Naked (without possessions) I came [into
> this world] from my mother's womb,
> And naked I will return there.
> The Lord gave and the Lord has taken away;
> Blessed be the name of the Lord."
> Through all this Job did not sin nor did he blame God."

God is Sovereign. God is Holy. God is Love. And He is my cup.

> "The Lord is my chosen and assigned portion, my cup;
> You hold and maintain my lot." Psalms 16:5 (AMPC).

Six
The Truck

―――――――――♡―――――――――

For You formed my innermost parts; You knit
me [together] in my mother's womb.
I will give thanks and praise to You, for I
am fearfully and wonderfully made;
Wonderful are Your works, And my soul knows it
very well. My frame was not hidden from You,
When I was being formed in secret, And intricately and
skillfully formed [as if embroidered with many colors]
in the depths of the earth. Your eyes have seen my
unformed substance; And in Your book were all written
The days that were appointed for me, When as yet
there was not one of them [even taking shape].
How precious also are Your thoughts to me, O God!
—Psalms 139: 13–17 (AMP)

D uring the detective's initial visit to the hospital, he discussed some of the legalities with Walt and me. One particular element I paid no attention to during his visit involved the truck Teagan drove at the time of the accident and her personal belongings. It was a few weeks after the accident before detectives would allow us and our insurance adjuster to see Teagan's truck. The city of Huntington Beach had it stored in one of their yards along with the drunk driver's vehicle, which hit her. Walt and I were hesitant to see her truck for fear of the unexpected. From the time of the accident, my mind had developed many visual scenarios. However, I still didn't know what to expect or how to quell my fear of seeing her vehicle. The police detective described how Teagan's personal belongings had scattered throughout the intersection. Her clothes, shoes, make-up, hair products, surfboard-almost everything she owned was in the back of the little Ford Ranger pick-up bed. The pick-up bed had a cover, a heavy cover that she usually locked. Apparently, she hadn't locked it before leaving her friend's house that evening or earlier that Tuesday morning.

Teagan was barely eighteen years old. She struggled to decide where to live and stayed between our home and her friends because she wanted to experience freedom from residing under our roof. Unfortunately, today's culture promotes promiscuity without consequences. Although Walt and I taught our children moral integrity from God's precepts, sometimes the pressure from society was weightier. I believe Teagan wanted to experience the same lifestyle as her brothers. Remembering her first birthday, her dad and I bought her a promise ring because we knew she was different, our little miracle God gave us. It was our way of personally dedicating her back to the Lord aside from church dedication. On her fifteenth birthday, we gave her the ring and told her its significance - the importance of keeping herself pure before the Lord until she married.

Before preparing for France, Teagan attended her second semester at the local Jr. College. At least, that was her desired plan before her accident. Teagan was a delight to one of her college teachers by Teagan's love for the language and how quickly she learned. She spoke beautifully. The French dialect just naturally rolled off my daughter's tongue as if it were her native language. Teagan had taken two years of French in high school because Spanish wasn't challenging enough. Her diligence to continue learning in college earned our daughter the opportunity to study in France the following summer. I was not surprised, but honored that her teacher chose her for this opportunity. Teagan excelled her entire life academically. She was in AVID (Advancement Via Individual Determination) during her elementary years. She was also a superior sportsman, having lettered her freshman year of high school. Surviving three older brothers gave her practical insight into handling certain types of conflict. Her dad was quite proud of his daughter, as she illustrated skills that even the boys had trouble displaying. In my opinion, her character was a combination of Walt's and my attributes (minus any bad stuff!). It was as if God had taken the best of me and the best of Walt and made a perfect little girl. People said she was beautiful, and yes, her appearance was stunning, but it was her heart that was exceptionally beautiful and the part of Teagan I delighted in. Teagan was musically inclined and also a talented drawing artist. Our daughter had an ear for music, so she taught herself to play the piano.

While in elementary school, she played a variety of instruments. She constantly challenged herself, starting with violin, cello, then bass. Imagine a four-foot sixth-grader moving around with a six-foot bass on her back! I recall having conversations with her about how the instruments she chose must fit in our vehicles! Next, if learning the string instruments wasn't enough, she ventured into the brass section. She began with trombone, moved on to French horn, but my favorite was the euphonium. It is a beautiful soft-sounding brass horn, and when Teagan played it, my heart melted with such pride and joy. I couldn't believe God had given me such a wonderful, talented, healthy, intelligent little girl.

I noticed her love of learning from when she was three years old. I taught her class in the children's program at our church for a few years when our children were in grade school. I saw how she would soak up Bible verses unlike any other child in her class of twenty students. Teagan was a bright, tenacious young lady who loved reading and eating veggies! In junior high, her talent progressed from music to drawing due to an inadequate music program at her school. I noticed she could look at an object or person, then sketch it from memory almost perfectly. Obviously, she was incredibly talented. I regret that I did not purposely harvest her talents for the Lord at church. However, I sensed He glorified Himself through her wherever she was. I wish I would have ignored other insignificant details of life to spend more time cultivating and expanding her God-given gifts for His purpose. Yet, all these qualities were negligible. I love Teagan because she belonged to me. She was mine. A beautiful gift God graciously gave me. She was my only daughter, who I was pleased with just because of who she was. It didn't matter what she accomplished or not. All her little accolades didn't define her. What defined her was that she belonged to me—God gave her to me.

I could now relate to God our Heavenly Father when He said to Jesus upon being baptized in water, "and behold, a voice from heaven said, "This is My beloved Son, in whom I am well-pleased and delighted!" Matthew 3:17 (AMP) God is a proud parent! He loves His one and only Son, Jesus. Teagan is our one and only beloved daughter, in whom I am delighted too! Coincidence or providence? It's through this perfect love that God sees us. It's not us in our sin, as the Bible describes as filthy rags, or through our proud achievements that God sees and loves us, but through His son, Jesus, who is perfect and sinless. Whoever loves and accepts Jesus, God accepts and receives as His own because Jesus loves them.

"If you declare with your mouth, "Jesus is Lord," and
believe in your heart that God raised Him from the
dead, you will be saved." Romans 10:9 (NIV)

"Therefore you are no longer a slave (bond servant) but
a son; and if a son, then [it follows that you are] an heir
of God through Christ." Galatians 4:7 (AMPC)

We become God's child, His son/daughter by birthright (a
spiritual adopted birthright), not by what we do or don't do. We
are given the King's robe, the robe of righteousness, because of
Jesus, not because we have earned it. Nothing we do will ever be
perfect enough to acquire such a great salvation. He was the perfect
sacrifice dying on the cross for our sins. Now, God no longer sees
us in our wretched sinful clothes with shame and guilt! No! He sees
us through His son, Jesus. We wear the guiltless, sinless, righteous
robe of Jesus on us! We have a right-standing with God because of
His Son. It's through that lens, the lens of mercy, compassion, and
fierce love, that Jesus graciously bestows on us that He was willing
to give up His life. This lens is what I now clearly see myself and
others through.

When it was time to gather our daughter's belongings at the
police yard, I hesitated during our walk to the vehicle. I remember
feeling fearful, slowly approaching the area where the tow truck
had dropped off her Ford Ranger. I tightly gripped Walt's arm with
my head down, and my eyes opened barely enough to see where I
was walking. After walking several yards, courageously, I looked up
and saw my daughter's truck. What I had seen bewildered me. We
approached her vehicle from behind. Her personal belongings were
placed in the bed of the truck stuffed in large trash bags as if her life
was garbage. That was a distraction and not what my heart wanted
to receive. I would not accept the garbage narrative because that's
a lie from the devil! Although the world may have discarded my

daughter and her belongings, that's not who she was. She was and still is the King's daughter, and all her material earthly possessions were just "stuff."

If we are not careful, we can lose focus or perspective on what is legitimate and important; we can lose the reverential fear of God. Jesus is the only true King. As believers, we need to be Kingdom-minded, having His eternal perspective and not our own.

> "And I say to you, My friends, do not be afraid of those
> who kill the body, and after that have no more that they
> can do. But I will show you whom you should fear: Fear
> Him who, after He has killed, has power to cast into hell;
> yes, I say to you, fear Him!" Luke 12:4–5 (NKJV)

Although I had Jesus' eternal kingdom perspective, my humanness struggled from the loss.

As my bewilderment drew me closer to see the truck, I noticed several things. The back window on the driver's side was crushed. In contrast, the passenger's side was completely intact, with not even a slight crack on the window from the other side. So as Walt was on the driver's side investigating the irreparable damage, I walked to the passenger's side. The passenger's side was undisputable whole; the back window, the front window shield, the door—it was as if there was no impact at all! Then my eyes peered toward my baby's side of the car. The truck's front and back driver's windshield were utterly shattered, the door's window was destroyed, and her door was smashed like a crumpled can of soda—the whole front side was demolished. The sovereign wonder of God kept Anthony whole, safe and preserved, while He allowed my daughter to be crushed and thrown from the vehicle. Was this coincidence? Or was it providence? I sensed in my spirit that God sent an angel to save Anthony from any harm because his time, his destiny, was not yet fulfilled. And if Anthony chose to see God's sovereign power and strength in protecting him, he would see God's fierce love for him and accept Him as his Lord and Savior. I hoped Anthony would not be angry and bitter or resentful to God for taking his friend Teagan. I hope Anthony will endure life's tragedies that we cannot understand or change, seek God's will and strength through life's circumstances, and learn to trust Him.

The concept of trusting reminds me of a song I sang as a little girl called, "His eye is on the sparrow." The lyrics reference the following scripture:

> "Are not two sparrows sold for a copper coin? And not one of them falls to the ground apart from your Father's will. But the very hairs of your head are all numbered. Do not fear therefore; you are of more value than many sparrows. Matthew 10:29-31 (NKJV)

The King has the last word. If He decrees death or life, it will be so.

Seven
The Key

I am He who lives, and was dead, and
behold, I **am** alive forevermore. Amen.
And I have the keys of Hades and of Death.
—Revelation 1:18 (NKJV)

It was a little over a year after Teagan's passing when I read a commentary by Joyce Meyers titled, "Leave the Past Behind." She was referencing the story of the impact on Joshua regarding Moses' death in Joshua chapter 1. The record indicates the Lord's instructions to Joshua to take Moses' place and lead His people, the Israelites, into the Promised Land. He made promises to Joshua and reminded him it was time to be strong and courageous. Joshua saw how God was with Moses.

I can imagine the loneliness, the sense of fear, and intimidation that may have swirled through Joshua's mind. I believe the enemy tried to keep him from moving forward after Moses' death—to keep Joshua from receiving and entering into the promised land, his destiny. Yet, I wondered if his experience of seeing God work on Moses' behalf helped build Joshua's faith. Despite the feelings and thoughts Joshua experienced, there were conditions that needed to be met. Joshua had to let go.

According to Scripture, the law of Moses allowed the Israelites thirty days to mourn. I'm sure there's practical reasoning behind this. However, it was nearly fifteen months after the passing of Teagan. I was still grieving over our loss of her and struggling to let go, wanting to obey the Lord and move forward. Letting go doesn't mean letting go of the person by means of memory or trying to forget about them. My mind and my heart missed and ached for Teagan to be with us, and I didn't want to let go of her memory and the way I felt about her. As days passed, I thought our daughter's memory and strong feelings would dissipate, but that is not true. My feelings for Teagan are still intense because of my never-ending love for her.

The lie that the enemy wants me to think is if I purposed to move on or let go—to obey God—I would lose my feelings and memories of her. The liar wants to distract me into believing this, thus keeping me (in mourning) from reaching my destiny and honoring the Lord. I also didn't want her to become my idol. If I focused on pleasing my feelings and kept mourning while making Teagan my number one priority, this would have put God in second place. I certainly wanted to make sure that my relationship with Jesus came first, my obedience to His Word and His calling.

When my Bible commentary mentioned, "Joshua would miss Moses, but he knew he had to obey God and move on." that is when I knew it was time for a change. The phrase hit me like a rock over the head. These moments are when you know God is trying to reach you, comfort you, and enlighten you. It precisely said what I was experiencing at that time. That's what Jesus does. His Holy Spirit speaks to us at critical moments since He knows the hidden secrets of our hearts. God knows what troubles us and brings them out of the dark places of our hearts and minds and shines His glorious light, the Spirit of Truth (John 16:13, AMPC), on those things to heal us. He brings healing and wholeness. He makes me stand. He plants my feet on the Rock. The Rock of my salvation, the cornerstone, Jesus.

I seriously hate mourning. It's emotionally exhausting. I mourned a lot when I was a child and young adult. It seemed as though people and the enemy himself, using certain circumstances, had taken advantage of my strengths and tried turning them into weaknesses. When I was young and naive, I allowed people to take advantage of the compassionate heart God gave me as they used it towards their selfish goals. Rather than respecting me, they benefited from me, leaving me feeling and thinking negative thoughts of myself. I felt helpless, victimized, used, abused, lonely, and a myriad of other demoralizing feelings that eventually turned to a bitter hatred towards people. Since I spent most of my childhood in church, this behavior was primarily directed to certain Christians. Individuals I thought I could trust. I found myself mourning over what I allowed people to take from me. I didn't know I could place boundaries on other people, protecting my heart, mind, and emotions.

Until losing Teagan, one of the most challenging and uncontrollable events in my life, as a teenager where I experienced mourning, was during my parent's divorce. The loss of family was devastating. It wasn't just one thing that was ripped from my life during this time, there were several. On Christmas Eve during my senior year of high school, my mother decided to pull me from attending, leave my father and move to Puerto Rico. I was only able to take a small number of clothes and personal items which would fit in one piece of luggage and leave my father. I had mourned bitterly for years and resented my mother. I always sensed their marriage was an unhealthy situation that could have been resolved. But what do I know? I was a kid. Nonetheless, it left me feeling abandoned, broken, and alone. I mourned the sudden loss of my father and the kindness he showed me. Since my mother was hardly ever kind to me, my father had seldom filled that area in my life. But now that was gone. I also mourned all familiar things, including my hometown, surroundings, friends, and friendships. I am grateful for the three friends who kept close touch with me and helped me during those painful years.

As a mother, I mourned when our first-born son, Jared, joined the military. I grieved when our teenage boys decided they didn't want to live within our boundaries, our house rules, and moved out, leaving their sister, Teagan, all alone. It was heartbreaking for me to see her go through her teenage years, through high school all alone. She was the baby sibling, so she was accustomed to living in a house full of people. I did my best to console our daughter by keeping her close to her dad and me and by encouraging and engaging with her. However, I could sense by her behavior that life wasn't the same, and she also seemed to be mourning. During her sophomore year, she did her best to overcome the complexities and attitudes of entitled, haughty, spoiled brat teenage students in her new school. Still, I saw her frustration, and I could tell she was hurting. She was lonely. Her heart was so generous, she naturally gravitated towards hurting people to console or encourage them. Teagan wouldn't share details with me, but I knew enough and saw how she was making a difference in someone else's life by just loving on them and meeting them where they were.

When Teagan passed away, I was not only mourning because I missed her, but I mourned for all of the missed opportunities to spend time with her in the future. She was only eighteen years old when her life began, and her life's journey was taken from her. As a mother wanting to protect her child, I couldn't do so. Teagan wasn't allowed to continue living her life glorifying God the way I think He purposed or destined. I thought this because of the vision I had of her as a young lady praying for people. This was her calling. It was a vision God gave me in 2008 of her and her brother while I was washing the car one day. I mourned because she couldn't walk in her calling the way God perfectly willed it to be. It broke my heart.

There's no correct way to mourn. There are healthy and unhealthy ways, but everyone is different, so we all mourn differently for various periods. Personally, I chose to take ahold of God's Word. He's the person I run to. He's been my anchor all my life.

> "[Now] we have this [hope] as a sure and steadfast
> anchor of the soul [it cannot slip and it cannot
> break down under whoever steps out upon it–a
> hope] that reaches farther and enters into [the very
> certainty of the Presence] within the veil,"
> Hebrews 6:19 (AMPC)

I've been through tumultuous periods in my life, this being one of them, and since He created me, He knows me best. He has shown Himself faithful and true to me, and there is no one else I would run to. That was my key. That is The Key!

Jesus is the Key!! All the anguish, confusion, and torment that had me questioning why He allowed Teagan to die was soothed by His loving words of comfort. It was His Word that soothed my spirit and my mind and filled my heart with such gratefulness.

> "In the beginning [before all time] was the Word
> (Christ), and the Word was with God, and the
> Word was God Himself." John 1:1 (AMPC)

> "Yes, though I walk through [the deep, sunless] valley of
> the shadow of death, I will fear or dread
> no evil, for You are with me;
> Your rod [to protect] and Your staff
> [to guide], they comfort me."
> Psalms 23:4 (AMPC)

Reading this with great attention, word for word, is very comforting. It assures me that I will go through some pretty tough, dark times in my life, but it's just a shadow. It cannot hurt me. I don't have to be afraid while going through these horrible, temporary seasons because God promised in His Word that He is with me, and He comforts me.

As a believer, it's a consolation when Jesus said, "And do not fear those who kill the body but cannot kill the soul; but rather fear Him who is able to destroy both soul and body in hell (Gehenna)." Matthew 10:28 (AMPC)

Basically, we don't need to fear men or what people may say or do to harm us, but we should fear God. We should have respect and possess a reverence for our Creator, our Redeemer, our Lord, and King! Why? Because He LOVES us! He doesn't want us to be distracted by all the horrible things done or being done to us. He wants us to focus on His love for us. Because it's His great love for us that will sustain us through hardships. It is His love for us that empowers us to overcome.

If you continue reading, Jesus puts things into perspective with His truth. He glorifies Himself as Creator when He says, "Are not two sparrows sold for a copper coin? And not one of them falls to the ground apart from your Father's will." Matthew 10:29 (NKJV) God knows our future. Nothing can harm us apart from His will. He knows! God knows us so well and cares for us so much; He even knows how many hairs each has on our head (or not)! (verse 30, NKJV) Meditate on that. Let that sink in. Marvel at the handiwork and the loving God He is, that He would care to count or just know the strands of hair we have on our heads—everyone's head!

I'm awestruck reading this, then in more profound awe of Him wanting to care about how many hairs I have on my head! Even if I pulled a small section of my hair right now and started to count each and every strand, it would take me a while, so I don't really care to know how many strands of hair I have in my head, but He does! There is no disrespect for bald people due to illness or some hereditary gene, but you get the gist of it. He cares—even for the minute details of our lives. Thus, Jesus closes with "Fear not then; YOU are of MORE VALUE than many sparrows." (vs31 AMPC).

In the hospital, while Teagan was lying in the hospital bed, it concerned me deeply whether her soul would be with Jesus. Contrary to what culture tells us, "Everyone goes to heaven if you're good.", is not correct. God's Word teaches us that Jesus is the only Way, "Jesus said to him, "I am the [only] Way [to God] and the [real] Truth and the [real] Life; no one comes to the Father but through Me." John 14:6 (AMP) Teagan did believe in God and had accepted Jesus as her Lord and Savior, and she was baptized with water. So I knew in my heart this was true, but the enemy was placing doubts in my mind. I needed a confirmation. I want to know that I know that I know. You know? More than wanting her alive and here with us, I wanted to know and make sure my daughter, her soul, would be with Him. When it was time to release Teagan, I pondered. I had sensed His will was not to restore her earthly body, yet to glorify Himself in a different manner. He chose not to raise her from the dead, but for us to be still and know that He is God (Psalm 46:10, NKJV). When I surrendered and laid my desire down, it was then when I started looking for His wonder. My heart was distraught, and I needed, we needed to know. It was our humanness.

The enemy of our soul likes to torment us. He has a field day distracting us with his lies. The Bible teaches us that Satan is the accuser/adversary of the brethren. (Revelation 12:10, AMPC) He's out to destroy each and every person. As believers in Jesus Christ as Lord and Savior, Satan cannot take possession of or in us, but he can attempt to harass our minds. He listens to the words of our mouths (only God knows our thoughts), our concerns and harasses us with them. If we believe certain lies from our legitimate concerns, they will grow like a weed in a beautiful garden of Truth and will choke and suffocate us. We need to take every negative "thought captive" as the Word teaches us in 2 Corinthians 10:5 (NKJV). And we need to be consistent in pushing back his antics. The adversary doesn't know our thoughts but enjoys blowing things out of proportion by whispering lies to us. Maybe not full-blown in our face, but maybe with half-truths, very subtle, like a snake. He's called the father of lies and a murderer. (John 8:44, NKJV) He is also called a thief and a robber.

> "The thief comes only in order to steal and kill and destroy. I came that they may have and enjoy life, and have it in abundance (to the full, till it overflows)."
> John 10:10 (AMPC)

There's a difference between a thief and a robber. This is why Jesus speaks of Satan being both. A thief unlawfully takes another person's property with the intention of not returning it. We are made in God's image; we belong to Him, His creation. So the thief will use stealth to try and lure us away from Him. Differencebetween. com states, "A thief conducts his operation in stealth when no one is around as he does not want to attract any attention." Meaning he doesn't want to announce to you, "Hey! I'm going to take you now!" in a loud voice. He doesn't want you to notice him or what he's doing. If you're not paying attention, Satan will use distractions to make you think one way while luring you away from God and having a relationship with God. It's a slow death.

On the other hand, a robber uses violence. He uses intimidation. He tries to put fear into you or make you think fearful thoughts as he tries to take what does not belong to him. As a believer, this is the violence I'm very familiar with.

So during our phase of concern for Teagan's salvation, the enemy tried to have a party by placing lies in our minds. Our thoughts and fears for her soul tormented us. Regardless of how much we pushed back, the harassment kept coming at us relentlessly. Then God stepped in, and His mercy took over. This was the wonder I was waiting for. All the while, God, our loving, gracious, merciful, all-knowing Father, understanding our hearts and minds, rescued us and gave us relief. The confirmation of knowing. This believer, Teagan's mom, was more concerned with the knowing (whether Teagan was with Jesus) than the why (Teagan wasn't with us).

One evening was brutal. Approximately a month after leaving the hospital, Walt couldn't sleep due to his grief. Restlessness from the pain consumed him, so he went to the couch in the living room of our small two-bedroom apartment. While I was in bed, finally sleeping, Walt stayed awake lying on the sofa, crying out to God. It must have been around 3 a.m., when suddenly, there she was. Walt saw Teagan! My husband mentioned he thought he was dreaming, but he wasn't asleep. Walt was awake when he saw two figures near our front door in the shadow. One was Teagan as she stepped out of the shadow and approached him; the other figure stayed back. Teagan was beautiful with her lovely big smile and dimples as she drew near Walt, kissed him on the forehead, and said, "I'm OK, Daddy." And then they disappeared. My husband said our daughter was dressed in a white gown, and her countenance was bright! Her hair was her usual dark brown tone, yet it had gold in it, strands of gold!

Scripture describes what we will look like:

"She has been permitted to dress in fine (radiant) linen, dazzling and white—for the fine linen is (signifies, represents) the righteousness (the upright, just, and godly living, deeds, and conduct, and right standing with God) of the saints (God's holy people)." Revelation 19:8 (AMPC)

"The royal daughter is all glorious within the palace; Her
clothing is woven with gold." Psalms 45:13 (NKJV)

"The King's daughter in the inner part [of the
palace] is all glorious; her clothing is inwrought
with gold." Psalms 45:13 (AMPC)

Teagan was in her heavenly body! I believe it's the same glorified
type of body that Jesus has and was a testament when He returned to
earth for forty days after His resurrection from dying on the cross!!
(Luke 24, Acts 1)

When I awoke and didn't see Walt in bed with me the following
day, I got up and found him on the couch. Assuming he had a
rough night, I moved beside him and snuggled next to him in a
sense to comfort him. Later that morning, he shared his experience
with me. From then on, we knew. We had peace and confidence
knowing Teagan was with our Lord Jesus. He has her right now in
His presence, and the enemy has no power to keep tormenting us.
Yes, the devil will attempt to get us off track once in a while to rob
us of our peace while we sleep. However, we continue to push back
harder with God's Truth by rebuking and reminding the evil one of
his destiny by speaking and confessing God's Word over Satan's lies
and schemes. We remember God's mercy. His mercy said, "No! I
hold the keys of death and hell, and I say No! You can't have Teagan.
I created Teagan; I love her, she is mine, and I have the last say!

I Am the Great I AM!"

That's His Fierce LOVE for all of us. That is His fierce love
for me.

Eight
The Courtroom

[It is that purpose and grace] which He now has
made known and has fully disclosed and made real
[to us] through the appearing of our Savior Christ
Jesus, Who annulled death and made it of no effect
and brought life and immortality (immunity from
eternal death) to light through the Gospel.
—2 Timothy 1:10 (AMPC)

The drunk driver (under the influence of drugs and alcohol) who hit our daughter's truck is named Darius. The officers and head detective who entered the little room at the hospital that first day eventually shared with Walt and me what had happened after the incident. They shared the miserable foggy weather condition Teagan drove in Huntington Beach. Because of the fog, our daughter drove cautiously through the intersection when she was violently hit. She was ejected from her vehicle when the other driver drove over ninety miles an hour upon impact. One of the 711 convenience store clerks decided to quit because the accident scene was so traumatizing. It was they who called 911 or the police that morning.

The dense fog made it difficult for the responding police officers, impairing their visibility to make quick judgments. When they approached the crime scene, only the victims were found. The miracle that happened was as one of the patrol officers was driving to the intersection, he noticed a person running away from the scene but towards the officer's direction. So the officer stopped to question the person running. That person was Darius Roberts. Was this coincidence or providence? I believe God had His hand in this situation.

Our final day in court was set for October 30, 2020, almost four years after the accident and many court hearings. In order for us to be at the courthouse by 9 a.m., Walt and I rose out of bed early, wondering what might happen and how things may go. We were not sure what to expect concerning the process of the courtroom setting or the behavior of those present, such as family members, the defendant, attorneys, and the judge.

That Friday October morning was sunny and relatively warm. However, the haze from recent local fires was consuming the clear air as the Santa Ana winds affected the atmosphere. The public wore facemasks or coverings and kept a distance of six feet apart due to the "pandemic" that consumed and distracted the nation during this season. You were frowned upon and labeled uncaring if you were against wearing face coverings. Stores prohibited people from entering and purchasing food and necessities unless they followed governing restrictions. Many people, little self-righteous gods, acting presumptuously voiced their uneducated opinions, chastising and judging people. There was an oppressing spirit over the earth—an atmosphere of division and hate. As time progressed, studies have shown that the virus subjected people to get vaccinated. I believe it was a way for confident leaders to control through fear and anxiety, rather than remedying the actual ill effects on the human body. As I have prayed and researched, I've discerned the devil's tactics to use these deadly intentions against God's creation. Sin in the hearts of wicked men provides for sinful behavior and death.

> "Therefore you have no excuse or justification, everyone of you who [hypocritically] judges and condemns others; for in passing judgment on another person, you condemn yourself, because you who judge [from a position of arrogance or self-righteousness] are habitually practicing the very same things [which you denounce]. And we know that the judgment of God falls justly and in accordance with truth on those who practice such things." Romans 2:1–2 (AMP)

As we entered the courthouse, there was so much tension. There was tension from the county sheriffs, who seemed agitated while still observant as they performed their duties. I sensed anxiousness from the lawyers and court personnel who were rushing, pressed for time in-between court cases or appointments due to standing in line for temperature checks. Court personnel double-checking I.D.'s from Walt and me, the public, were very watchful not to go against useless covid-19 rules and procedures. Despite the chaos and confusion, Walt and I lived in peace. Once we found our courtroom on the 11th floor, we had to wait a while due to another court case mishap which placed us in the second position. Walt and I went to the cafeteria to split a breakfast burrito and coffee to stay nourished until they called us back to the courtroom.

Finally, at 10:42 a.m., Patricia, with the Homicide Victim Services, which works with the district attorney's department, called for us. Patricia has been instrumental in keeping us informed about the go-betweens, the District Attorney's office, and us. It was time. We promptly made our way to the 11th floor and entered Judge King's courtroom C45. There must have been fifteen or so people total in the courtroom. About half was the court staff, not including the D.A., defense attorney, and Darius, the defendant. The seats were marked with red tape where people were not allowed to sit. Walt and I had to sit a row and two chairs apart. Really? We've been married for over thirty years. We sleep, eat, and work together. Do they think this ridiculous seating requirement will stop us from getting this made-up virus from each other? It defied common sense and all practical logic. It was absolutely heartbreaking not being able to sit close to my husband during this heart-wrenching process. Darius finally pled guilty to manslaughter, serving ten years in addition to the two years he had already served. That sentence is not much time to pay the penalty for the death of our precious daughter, but God is merciful, and we wanted what was just in His eyes.

During a pleading or a court case hearing, the victim or the family/friends of the victim are awarded time to speak. It's a way of closure for many. For us, Teagan's family, it was partial closure. When the District Attorney, Dan, asked us to give our victim impact statement, I chose to have Danielle, Anthony's mother, read her statement first. She started with Anthony's letter, which he had written about seven months after the accident. It was fresh and raw in his memory, and I could feel the deep emotion in his words. While Danielle read his statement, it brought back visual, horrific memories of Teagan lying in the hospital bed. I lost it. I was swept back to the most horrible time of our lives, and I wept bitterly. My mind and body were so full of distress and emotion that I had difficulty gathering my composure to exercise self-control to share my statement when it was time to speak.

When Danielle finished her statements, it was our turn to take the stand. As I sat in the witness stand with paper in hand, Walt sitting behind me (due to covid restrictions), I cried profusely while trying to contain myself to start speaking. The judge kindly urged me to take my time. I blinked and tried to brush away my tears to read my letter. Then, as I began to read, I felt strength rising from inside of me. The context of my letter was not about me or how I felt, or what I had lost. It was all about God. His character. I spoke of His sovereignty, creativity, love, mercy, and most of all, forgiveness.

Towards the middle of my one-page letter, the progressing strength I felt inside me gave me an unexplainable boldness. I had passion in my voice, tears in my eyes, and the convicting, loving spirit in my heart which conveyed what needed to be said. It was what God wanted them to hear. The bottom line: the Lord forgave us from our sins, so we forgave Darius for the death of our daughter. During the hearing, I didn't know our statement's impact on people listening as they sat in the courtroom. All I knew was what I had to say and do. And that was to stand. Stand firmly on God's word declaring forgiveness to Darius before God in front of witnesses.

After I spoke, Walt made a short statement directly to Darius, with compassion and understanding that we understood it was not his intent to hurt our daughter. Walt has always tried to place himself in the other person's shoes. Remember the incident with the elderly lady when she ran into our car? Merciful. That's how my husband spoke, and I was proud of my husband, once again. He had told me earlier that he didn't have anything to say other than "I forgive you." Still, when it came time, Walt spoke from the love and passion of his heart, as a father—like our heavenly Father would—to Darius, a young man who respectfully listened.

I knew it was the Holy Spirit speaking through Walt. I know my husband, and I know the Holy Spirit, and it was the Holy Spirit that gave Walt the words that Darius needed to hear from a man—a God-fearing man. Walt illustrated how a man should courageously stand for what is right and just in the eyes of the Lord. In Matthew 10:19–20, Mark 13:11, and Luke 12:12 (AMPC), the Bible teaches us that the Holy Spirit will give us or teach us what to say in that very hour. God can use us effectively to bring glory to Himself and bless others when we humble ourselves.

After returning to our seats, the defense team's turn was to speak. Darius' grandmother spoke on behalf of Darius and herself, expressing how sorry they were. As she asked for forgiveness, I couldn't possibly bear to look at her in that instant. I slithered down in my seat and found it necessary to hide my face to avoid looking at her. I felt hurt and angry since I did not want to hear her apologize, but instead from Darius himself. Even though I was presumptuous in my thinking, which made me feel angry, I still believed it was inappropriate. Darius is a grown man who made his own decision. Having negative thoughts, I sat alone and cried when Walt noticed I was emotionally distressed. Feeling compassion, my thoughtful husband asked the D.A., who was seated directly in front of Walt, if we could sit together so that he could comfort me. Looking at the judge, the D.A. said, "yes" and with the judge's nodded permission, I moved across the aisle to sit with Walt. As I expressed my negative thoughts to Walt, he reminded me that it was not the grandmother but rather some other relative who convinced Darius to change his plea to *not guilty*, which adversely affected and prolonged the case. Walt's reminder changed my attitude, and my heart softened. I still couldn't look at Darius' grandmother, but I received her confession and remorse. I anticipated Darius' statement and firmly felt that an apology was not complete unless I heard what Darius had to say.

When Darius' grandmother sat down, the defense attorney offered some comments to the court, then asked if Darius could speak. Hence, the judge allowed her request, calling him to the stand to read his statement. The defense prefaced Darius' statement mentioning Darius was nervous. I don't know Darius and couldn't tell if he was nervous based on his behavior. He stood and walked to the stand assisted by the bailiff, heeding to the judge's instructions. Darius' confession and apology were brief. He was sorry for making the decision that led to Teagan's death and confessed if he could trade places with Teagan, he would. Additionally, he was grateful for the forgiveness and graciousness we, the Wehrmann's, extended to him. Further comments expressed the same idea of remorse, but overall his statement was short and straightforward. His voice seemed calm and meek, but his body language lacked visible signs of remorse or emotion. Darius did not offer any excuses or reasoning in his statement. Due to my perplexity, I didn't think of it at the time, but I wonder if those were Darius's own words? Perhaps he meant what he said yet needed a little direction in keeping the statement and apology simple. I was curious if Darius had assistance with prepping his speech.

During one of our last Zoom meetings and before the final court date with the prosecuting team, I felt led to ask the district attorney if Darius showed any remorse. Dan had replied, "Yes. And as a matter-of-fact Darius wanted to reach out to us, Teagan's family, but for legal reasons he was advised not to." When Dan mentioned this, I broke down in tears. It's what I needed to hear. We had already forgiven Darius, but it gave me hope upon hearing Dan's comments. Somehow, it brought reconciliation and healing. However, this confession seemed elusive unless I heard from Darius directly.

Experiencing our tragedy gave me a heightened awareness of God's precepts and how the Holy Spirit worked those teachings within and through me. They're true. When we choose to follow His divine principles—when we obey His Word—our Creator blesses us. It falls in line with the law of sowing and reaping. I call them *commanded blessings*, as they provide an unbelievable and unimaginable peace that I cannot put into words.

"Thou wilt keep Janette in perfect peace, whose mind is stayed on thee: because Janette trusteth in thee." Isaiah 26:3 (KJV). I like to make it personal, so I substitute the "him and he" pronouns and replace them with my name or the name of the person I'm praying for.

Culture provokes us to respond retaliatorily when someone hurts us (intensionally or not). The Word teaches us to confess our sins and to forgive. Forgiveness is a choice, not a feeling. It's a choice to surrender and trust God to avenge on our behalf.

> "Beloved, do not avenge yourselves, but rather give
> place to wrath; for it is written, "Vengeance is Mine, I
> will repay," says the Lord." Romans 12:19 (NKJV)

Surrendering to God doesn't release the offense nor the offender—they're still accountable before God and man for what they did or said and will reap the consequences. Instead, it releases us from bondage the offense can have when we forgive, bringing healing and restoration. Restoring the relationship, the peace you have with God, your Creator, Lord, and King. No matter how gut-wrenching it feels, we need to crucify our will—our offenses, our self-righteousness—the same way Christ bore our sins, our offenses on the cross. When the opportunity presents itself, verbally confessing forgiveness to the offender or saying, "I forgive you." sheds light on and brings life to the situation—even if they don't ask for it. This deed takes humbling ourselves, showing mercy and love, hopefully causing the offender to repentance.

> "If your enemy is hungry, give him bread to eat;
> And if he is thirsty, give him water to drink;
> For in doing so, you will heap coals of fire upon his head,
> And the Lord will reward you." Proverbs 25:21–22 (AMP)

> "But if your enemy is hungry, feed him; if he is thirsty, give
> him a drink; for by doing this you will heap burning coals
> on his head. Do not be overcome and conquered by evil,
> but overcome evil with good." Romans 12:20–21 (AMP)

When we knowingly offend someone—purposely hurt someone by overstepping our boundaries—we dishonor God. We need to lay down our pride and confess our sins, our trespasses. When we submit to His will, certain things happen:

- **Confessing exposes sin.** Sin likes to stay hidden. It will give excuses or reasoning, practical or not, for protecting itself from the Spirit of Truth. It's self-serving, self-preserving, selfish, manipulative, proud, and promotes anger, which leads to hatred. It dwells and thrives in ignorance and complacency. It acts victimized. The eyes of sin look within and wait for the next opportune moment of a person's will to continue in a pattern of staying hidden, thus creating another link in the chain of bondage. Fortunately, darkness cannot hide in the light. Light (Jesus) exposes whatever hides in the dark (sin). Genesis 1:3 (AMPC) reads, "And God said,…." He spoke, He confessed, "Let there be light; and there was light." Merriam-Webster's dictionary meaning of confessing states:

  1. To tell or *make known*
  2. To acknowledge (sin) to God
  3. To declare faith in: Profess
  4. To give evidence of
  5. Admit, Own

So God made known that there was darkness by speaking Light (Spirit of Truth). "God saw that the light was good (pleasing, useful) and He affirmed (validated, testify or declare) and sustained (supports, nourishes; to support as truth, legal or just) it; and God separated the light [distinguishing it] from the darkness." Genesis 1:4 (AMP). I love the Amplified Bible version's use of "affirmed and sustained" (defined by Merriam-Webster's dictionary) to magnify the majestic, authoritative sovereignty of God. I enjoy digging deep into God's Word—passage by passage, word by word, piece by piece—because it has such meaning and depth to it! The Light, which is spiritual truth, is manifested in our physical realm to attribute in many ways.

- **Confessing honors God.** It validates the work of the Cross. It pleases Him. It exalts Him. It brings power to Jesus' name and the power of His resurrection. It recognizes the authority of the Cross. Pride crumbles as it submits, by laying the offense down, letting it die with Jesus at the cross, never to be brought up again, by conversation or reminders within our thoughts. Through confession, the offense no longer has power or control over the offender. Releasing the offender from any stronghold or bondage the enemy of our souls, Satan, may have or try to have on them.

Confessing releases the offender from judgment because Jesus bore all the sins of the world when He lovingly sacrificed His own life so that we may live.

> "For God so [greatly] loved and dearly prized the world, that He [even] gave His [One and] only begotten Son, so that whoever believes and trusts in Him [as Savior] shall not perish, but have eternal life. For God did not send the Son into the world to judge and condemn the world [that is, to initiate the final judgment of the world], but that the world might be saved through Him. Whoever believes and has decided to trust in Him [as personal Savior and Lord] is not judged [for this one, there is no judgment, no rejection, no condemnation]; but the one who does not believe [and has decided to reject Him as personal Savior and Lord] is judged already [that one has been convicted and sentenced], because he has not believed and trusted in

the name of the [One and] only begotten Son of God [the
One who is truly unique, the only One of His kind, the
One who alone can save him]." John 3:16–18 (AMPC)

"No one takes it away from Me, but I lay it down
voluntarily. [I put it from Myself.] I am authorized and
have power to lay it down (to resign it) and to give it up,
and I am authorized and have power to take it back again.
These are the instructions (orders) which I have received
[as My charge] from My Father." John 10:18 (AMPC)

- **Confessing heals.** It brings peace to our weary souls and
  restoration to our relationship with God and others. It starts
  binding up open wounds, sometimes immediately.

"Then your light will break out like the dawn,
And your healing (restoration, new
life) will quickly spring forth;
Your righteousness will go before you [leading
you to peace and prosperity], The glory of
the Lord will be your rear guard."
Isaiah 58:8 (AMP)

We sometimes forget or don't want to accept the fact that we are
all connected—perfectly woven in the image of God.

"Then God said, "Let Us (Father, Son, Holy Spirit)
make man in Our image, according to Our likeness
[not physical, but a spiritual personality and moral
likeness]; and let them have complete authority over
the fish of the sea, the birds of the air, the cattle, and
over the entire earth, and over everything that creeps
and crawls on the earth." Genesis 1:26 (AMP)

Whether we choose to believe it, God's likeness is in all of us. It's true. Whether you are a child of God, by accepting Jesus as your Lord and Savior, or you're currently not, it doesn't matter. God has created us; thus, we are all loved by Him. Therefore, when we knowingly (and unknowingly) offend by not respecting others for selfish reasons, it profoundly hurts the heart of God. The concept is pretty simple:

What Jesus did for EVERYONE	What believers in Jesus should do for each other	
We are sinners and offend God when we sin/disobey Him, His precepts. We were born into judgement = no relationship with God. Romans 5:12–13 (AMP) John 3:18 (AMP) 1 John 5:17 (AMP)	**Believers:** *Knowingly*, you offended someone—you purposed in your heart and mind to hurt someone else.	**Believers:** *Unknowingly* you offended someone, or you think your actions/words didn't offend someone.
God forgave us from our sin when Jesus offered up himself as a sacrifice. Luke 23:34 (KJV) Romans 5:10–11 (AMP)	You, the offender, need to go to the person you offended and **confess** your (specific) sin/offense to them. Go apologize! Make peace with them.	The offended need to go to the offender who sinned and tell them (**confess**) of the offender's wrongdoing. It doesn't matter how the offender responds, you need to obey. Matthew 18:15-17
Unless we **repent** (turning from our sinful nature/ disobedient ways) thus understanding there is NOTHING we can do from our own works/sacrifices— GRACE, to have a relationship with God/our Creator, and we: 1. ***Acknowledge*** and ***Confess*** with our mouths that Jesus is Lord, and 2. ***Believe*** in our hearts that God raised Jesus from the dead, *we will be saved.* Matthew 18:3 (AMP) Romans 10:8-13 (AMP) Romans 6:23 (AMP)	"So if you are presenting your offering at the altar, and *while* there you remember that your brother has something [such as a grievance or legitimate complaint] against you, leave your offering there at the altar and go. First make peace with your brother, and then come and present your offering." Matthew 5:23–24 (AMP) 1 John 1:9 (AMP) James 5:16 (AMP)	"If your brother sins, go and show him his fault in private; if he listens *and* pays attention to you, you have won back your brother. But if he does not listen, take along with you one or two others, so that EVERY WORD MAY BE CONFIRMED BY THE TESTIMONY OF TWO OR THREE WITNESSES. If he pays no attention to them [refusing to listen and obey], tell it to the church; and if he refuses to listen even to the church, let him be to you as a Gentile (unbeliever) and a tax collector." Matthew 18:15–17

We are now (that very moment) restored to God = We have a relationship with God, through His son Jesus—Free Gift of salvation, thus having eternal life! It's that simple. Now, you are considered a believer, follower of Jesus Christ, son/daughter of God! Romans 6:23 (AMP) 1 John 5:11–12 (AMP)	If you want God to forgive you from your sin, you first must go to your brother and ask for forgiveness. No matter how they respond, you need to obey. God is watching and He knows the hearts and thoughts of every person. If the offended receives you, then it's a win-win. Your relationship with the offended and with God has been restored. If the offended does not receive your sincere apology, God will deal with them. You've done your part to obey, now God will forgive you. ***All has been forgotten!*** Move on!	When we forgive, we give up our flesh (our pride, our ego, our selfishness, our sin) the way Jesus did at the cross for us even though He was perfect and sinless. Matthew 18:21-22

When the final judgment was complete, and the hearing concluded at the courthouse, everyone exited from inside the courtroom to the hallway. The trial was over. The feeling was strange, like a feeling of being lost. I thought to myself, *Now what do we do?* Walt and I stood in the hallway giving our regards to the prosecuting team when I noticed a small group of people gradually surrounding us. The unforeseen attention felt strange, and I struggled with it. I didn't want attention. I wanted to go home. I soon realized it was the magnetic attraction of Jesus—His love and mercy—which drew them near.

Darius' grandmother was one of them. When I looked at her, I saw a broken, sorrowful little girl with tears in her eyes. She respectfully approached me cautiously, not knowing what else to say to me, but tried somehow to convey how sorry she was. I didn't care about covid restrictions or what anyone else around me thought. That woman needed to feel loved, so I pushed the legal boundaries and grabbed hold of her and hugged her as a momma bear would hug her cubs. Afterward, we exchanged a few words then Walt and I walked a few steps towards the elevators. While waiting for the elevator, a beautiful, tall, blonde, confident-looking woman approached us, tapping me on the shoulder. I gathered she was a lawyer of some sort, holding onto her briefcase. When I looked up at her, all she could muster up to say was, "God bless you." as she tried holding back her tears. Just then, the elevator rang open, and she quickly walked into it. As I was preparing to follow her, Walt pulled me back and said, "Let her go alone." We didn't want to interfere with her encounter with God.

God wants people to know how much He loves them!! He wants them to know they have been forgiven. People need to see what true forgiveness looks like. Despite what we've been through, what we've done, or what we've heard, the truth is, without Jesus in our lives, we'll never be able to experience the incredible, amazing love and forgiveness of the Father. He wants us to know that all we have to do is believe in our hearts that He loves us! Jesus already took our sins and guilt away at the cross! The truth is death was annulled—like it never existed—so that we may live through the resurrected power of Jesus Christ here on earth. That's the good news! That's the gospel of Christ!

"This righteousness of God comes through faith in Jesus Christ *for all those [Jew or Gentile] who believe [and trust in Him and acknowledge Him as God's Son].* There is no distinction, since all have sinned and continually fall short of the glory of God, and are being justified [declared free of the guilt of sin, made acceptable to God, and granted eternal life] as a gift by His [precious,

undeserved] grace, through the redemption [the payment
for our sin] which is [provided] in Christ Jesus,"
Romans 3:22–24 (AMP)

"'that if you confess with your mouth the Lord
Jesus and believe in your heart that God has raised
Him from the dead, you will be saved. For with
the heart one believes unto righteousness, and with
the mouth confession is made unto salvation."
Romans 10:9–10 (NKJV)

"Jesus said to him, "I am the Way and the
Truth and the Life. No one comes to the Father
except through Me." John 14:6 (NKJV)
[It is that purpose and grace] which He now has made
known and has fully disclosed and made real [to us] through
the appearing of our Savior Christ Jesus, *Who annulled death
and made it of no effect* and brought life and immortality
(immunity from eternal death) to light through the Gospel.
2 Timothy 1:10 (AMCP)

A few days after our final day in court, I was surprised to hear
that Dan, the District Attorney, and his team wanted to have a
meeting. Walt and I discussed and questioned, "What could he
possibly discuss with us since everything was complete?" During
our meeting, we learned that even the judge had an encounter with
God's almighty love! Dan explained when he was called into the
judge's chambers after the hearing to find the judge in a compelling
position withholding his emotions. Dan was so choked up that it
was difficult to understand all he said during our meeting. Still,
nonetheless, we knew that the Holy Spirit, the love of Christ, had
gotten ahold of Dan's heart and the judges too! That just amazed
me. He got to the judge's heart.

Darius needed to know we forgave him so his guilt and shame would have no effect, and his heart and mind would be in peace. We needed to hear that he was genuinely sorry so that no resentment, anger, or harsh feelings would take place in our hearts, but rather peace. This is God's providence—**His Fierce Love**.

Nine
Teagan's Heart

Greater love has no one than this, than to
lay down one's life for his friends.
—John 15:13 (NKJV)

I believe it was Sunday, February 19, 2017, when we saw our daughter for the last time. I didn't want to leave her. I didn't want to abandon her or let her think I had abandoned her and didn't love her. I couldn't bear the thought of letting her go. Yes, it was selfish of me, but I had a desperate need to see her, despite the horrible condition her body was in as she lay motionless in the hospital bed. I didn't want to let her go. I knew that this was it, and I couldn't keep her to myself anymore. Although the doctors pronounced her death on Thursday, February 16, the machines were keeping Teagan's body alive until her eldest brother arrived from deployment. The hospital staff, including a representative from Donate Life, kept their eyes on us. They waited for an appropriate time to approach Walt and me to discuss and obtain our approval on how to proceed with Teagan's body.

Teagan was a legal adult when she passed away. She voted in the last presidential election. She was able to purchase things and do things without our consent. If the hospital staff wanted to, they could have disregarded us as her parents and made whatever decisions they deemed necessary. Part of me thinks the hospital did when they couldn't identify her and called her "Sugar Doe." The truck registration was in my name with a P.O. Box address, but what about her driver's license? Perhaps the ambulance took Teagan to the hospital while the police gathered her personal items from the street intersection. I believe the hospital took the opportunity to study Teagan's body and work on her brain to possibly save her. However, after Walt and I looked at the truck, we knew full well that our daughter had passed when she was struck by the drunk driver's vehicle.

Soon after Teagan's celebration of life ceremony, we learned UCI Douglas hospital or UCI Medical Center is a major research hospital, a teaching hospital for the University of California, Irvine School of Medicine. Her death certificate says February 16, but we know it was on the 15th at approximately 3:30 in the morning when our loving Lord swooped her into His arms. Donate Life works well with hospitals like these. I believe they take the John/Jane Doe body parts and use them for either research or to save other lives.

Throughout the duration of Teagan's time in the hospital, we didn't leave her out of our sight, except for an hour or two each day to go home, eat, shower, and change clothes. I believe the love we showed for Teagan and our responses and conduct with the staff and representatives gave us favor with them. When Donate Life approached us, they shared their research and organ donations options. As Teagan's parents, we didn't want to share any part of her, but as we placed ourselves in the recipients' shoes, our hearts were hard-pressed to sacrifice her organs to someone in need, giving someone a second chance to live. The representative reminded us which of Teagan's organs were salvable, as many were severely damaged. The doctors could only save a few of her vital organs: one kidney, a portion of her liver, and remarkably her entire heart. Teagan's beautiful heart remained whole. Jesus saved her spiritual, loving heart and made her whole when she entered into heaven, and at the same time, Jesus kept her physical heart whole to preserve life for another. Walt and I knew the spiritual condition of our daughter's heart, and we knew she would be willing to help another, just as she did when given opportunities while she was alive.

Teagan made a positive impact wherever she went. She stood up for people when they were downtrodden, gave words of encouragement to hopeless schoolmates, respected homeless people at her work when co-workers would speak disrespectfully to them. It's no wonder there were a large group of people from different areas throughout Southern California at a special going-away ceremony which Anthony so lovingly held for Teagan at the unique spot on the beach where they used to surf. She had shared her heart with different ethnic groups of various ages and classes of people. They all came to say their goodbyes to Teagan, and some of them wanted to share their experiences and how fond they were of Teagan with her father and me. They held single roses or flowers in their hands as one by one released them off the jetty into the sea. I was in awe of how many people's lives she touched. It was an honor to see my daughter's heart and it's positive effect on so many different people.

When Walt and I agreed to share Teagan's organs with others, the Donate Life rep walked us through the steps of turning over her body from the hospital's possession to the organization's doctors and medical staff to prepare her for the operations to take place. Walking away was beyond difficult and painful. Even though we knew our daughter was with her Heavenly Father, the pain of not having her with us, her earthly parents and family, left a huge void.

One of the most challenging things a parent can do is let their child go. We don't want them to grow up. We want their innocent little preciousness to stay young and helpless so that they stay under our wings and do not get hurt. When adolescents, we don't want to see their hearts broken; as young adults, we don't want to see them leave our homes. But when the life cycle gets cut short, those temporary losses of growing pains stop. There's no more connection, no more relationship. It just vanishes, leaving a gaping hole in your heart. There is nothing you can do to fill it, nor anyone to replace it. No matter how many pictures or videos you watch of your child who has passed, trying to hold on to them as you sense your memory of them slipping away, nothing you do will fill their place.

When I struggle with this feeling, I remember what the Lord told me one day in 2017. He said to me, "I feel this way when people reject Me, God their Creator, their Heavenly Father. It's like losing a child. It's an eternal void that can never be filled." God grieves over losing His creation, male and female made in His image, when they refuse to accept His love, His forgiveness to be restored to Him and have a relationship with Him. It was a heart-wrenching moment of severance both Father and Son experienced at a cost that no one can repay when Jesus bore all the sins of the world upon Himself at the cross and was separated from God the Father.

What Adam didn't do in the Garden of Eden, Jesus did at the cross. Adam's disobedience allowed sin into this world which led to [eternal] death, but Jesus' (God-in-flesh) obedience at the cross brought life. He bridged the gap and saved us from our sins so that we, His creation, would be restored back to Him.

> "So then as through one trespass [Adam's sin] there resulted
> condemnation for all men, even so through one act of
> righteousness there resulted justification of life to all men.
> For just as through one man's disobedience [his failure
> to hear, his carelessness] the many were made sinners, so

through the obedience of the one Man the many will be
made righteous and acceptable to God and brought into
right standing with Him." Romans 5:18-19 (AMP)

Thank you Jesus for willing to pay my penalty for the sins I committed, so that I may have right standing with God and have a relationship with my Heavenly Father—forever!

So I ask you, "Were these experiences just a *Coincidence or His Providence?*"

- February 15, 2017: The date Teagan was hit by the car, the real date she passed away. *The number fifteen in Hebrew represents <u>REST</u>: which implies salvation, healing, ascension, redemption. (Biblestudy.org)*
- February 16, 2017: The date the doctors pronounced Teagan dead. *The number sixteen is symbolic of <u>LOVE</u> and loving. (Biblestudy.org)*
- The Fog: that was so thick Teagan and others couldn't see through it. *Was God's visible presence—His Shekinah glory—ushering her into His heavenly realm?*
  "And the LORD went before them by day in a *<u>pillar of a cloud</u>*, to lead them the way;"
  Exodus 13:21 (KJV)
- The Truck: how it was hit and spared Anthony's life.
  "For He will give His angels [especial] charge over you to accompany *and* defend *and <u>preserve you</u>* in all your ways [of obedience and service]." Psalm 91:1 (AMPC)
- The Cross: the little window with a pane shaped like a cross.
  "Then Jesus said to His disciples, "If anyone wishes to follow Me [as My disciple], he must deny himself [set aside selfish interests], and *<u>take up his cross [expressing a willingness to endure whatever may come]</u>* and follow Me [believing

in Me, conforming to My example in living and, if need be, suffering or perhaps dying because of faith in Me]." Matthew 16:24 (AMP)

- The Word from the chaplain: *"Be still and know that I am God."*
- The Cup: the reminder/*confirmation* from the Word the chaplain spoke:

  "Be still and know (recognize, understand) that *I am* God. (If you read from the first verse it says, "God is our refuge and *strength* (mighty and impenetrable), *a very present* and well-proved help in trouble.) Psalm 46:10(AMP)

- The Confessions: strangely, a handful of young women and other adults, filled with sorrow and repentance in their hearts came up to me (seeking forgiveness) not looking to console me, but rather to say they were sorry for their behavior towards our daughter. The loving, convicting power of the Holy Spirit brings us to repentance so that we may be restored into having fellowship with Jesus.

  "For *godly sorrow produces repentance* leading to salvation, not to be regretted;"

  II Corinthians 7:10 (NKJV)

- Jesus' Fierce Love Attraction: People, like the judge, the officer, and others, who were affected by the love of Christ Jesus as God *drew them near* to Him.

  "No one is able to come to Me unless the Father Who sent Me *attracts and draws him and gives him the desire to come to Me*, and [then] I will raise him up [from the dead] on the last day." John 6:44(AMPC)

- Teagan's Heart: the only *whole and complete* vital organ in her body. The core of her being, bringing life physically to another. It is also her spiritual heart, that is whole and complete in heaven, which impacted people bringing life to them along her life's journey.

- Five days: I've read the Biblical meaning of the number five symbolizes _God's grace_. (Biblestudy.org) God's grace, His unmerited favor and power, was upon us during the five days we were at the hospital with Teagan.

  "For out of His fullness (abundance) we have all received [all had a share and we were all supplied with] one grace after another and spiritual blessing upon spiritual blessing and even favor upon favor and gift [heaped] upon gift." John 1:16 (AMPC)

- Three and a half years: Three is a picture of completeness— the number of resurrection. (Biblestudy.org) It was the number of years the King carried me as I felt His tangible presence—His love. Similarly, it was the same amount of time, Jesus ministered on this earth, before His death and resurrection.

Teagan is my one-and-only daughter—
Jesus is God's one-and-only son.

Without a doubt in my mind I can
irrefutably say it was **providence.**

That is King Jesus' *Fierce Love*! That is the Heart of the Father.

"PRAISE THE Lord! *Sing to the Lord a new song*, praise
Him in the assembly of His saints! Let Israel rejoice in Him,
their Maker; let Zion's children triumph and be joyful in their
King! Let them praise His name in chorus and choir and with
the [single or group] dance; let them sing praises to Him with
the tambourine and lyre! For the Lord takes pleasure in His
people; *He will beautify the humble with salvation and
adorn the wretched with victory*. Let the saints be joyful
in the glory and beauty [which God confers upon them]; let
them sing for joy upon their beds. Let the high praises of God
be in their throats and a two-edged sword in their hands,"
Psalm 149:1–6(AMPC)

My new song: "**Teagan's with my Lord. My baby and the King.**"

The heaviness of sorrow can be overwhelming,
especially when things are quiet, when we lay our
heads to rest. Painful memories full of regrets.
Let them all subside and kneel before the King.
Yes! I choose to praise you Lord—my baby is with the King!
No more heartache, no more sorrow, no deception.
Dance sweetheart, dance! Dance before His
Majesty—Dance before your King!
How lovely, how radiant, how beautiful you are.
Dance, my sweet Teagan—Dance before your King.
Written on December 29, 2017

You'll always be my mom-luv, my sonshine, my Sugar-Doe.

Love, Fierce Love

"Love endures with patience *and* serenity, love is kind *and* thoughtful, and is not jealous *or* envious; love does not brag and is not proud *or* arrogant. It is not rude; it is not self-seeking, it is not provoked [nor overly sensitive and easily angered]; it does not take into account a wrong *endured*. It does not rejoice at injustice, but rejoices with the truth [when right and truth prevail]. Love bears all things [regardless of what comes], believes all things [looking for the best in each one], hopes all things [remaining steadfast during difficult times], endures all things [without weakening]. **Love never fails** [it never fades nor ends].
1 Corinthians 13:4–8 (AMP)

"The one who does not love has not become acquainted with God [does not and never did know Him], for **God is love.** [He is the originator of love, and it is an enduring attribute of His nature.] By this the love of God was displayed in us, in that God has sent His [One and] only begotten Son [the One who is truly unique, the only One of His kind] into the world so that we might live through Him. In this is love, not that we loved God, but that He loved us and sent His Son to be the propitiation [that is, the atoning sacrifice, and the satisfying offering] for our sins [fulfilling God's requirement for justice against sin and placating His wrath]. Beloved, if God so loved us [in this incredible way], we also ought to love one another."
1 John 4:8–11 (AMP)

If you want to receive and experience the love of
King Jesus, simply read these words out loud:

Jesus, I need you.
I recognize my sin has kept me from
experiencing your fierce love for me.
Please forgive me and come into my heart, my life.
I believe You are the Son of the Living God and
You died on the cross for my sins and was raised from the dead,
so that I may have a relationship with You.
And now, I believe in You, Your Spirit lives in my heart.
I know I will live with You forever.
Thank you, Jesus.
Amen

If you made a decision to accept and follow Jesus as your
Lord and Savior, this is really good news for you to share!

I would love to hear from you!

janette@thewehrmannfoundation.org

Photos

Our Final Family Photo with Teagan
January 2016

The Cup

Teagan holding her nieces bday cake

The Wehrmann's Impact Statement

October 23, 2020
Case#: 18WF0373

Dear Honorable Judge Richard M. King,

Teagan Rylee Wehrmann, born September 20th, 1998 is our only daughter. She is the youngest of our four beautiful children.

We can share the wonderful person she was while living with us and the positive impact she made in her family's lives, but more profoundly, how Teagan touched the lives of those around her is a testimony of her character. A testimony of God's love for each of us. Upon her passing, many of her friends or acquaintances approached her father and I sharing different stories of how compassionate Teagan was towards them. How she treated them and would go out of her way for them. I personally love the story she told me when while working at Del Taco the other employees would make fun and mistreat a particular homeless person. Her valiant spirit would not tolerate such mistreatment as she spoke up against their unjustly behaviors and attitudes while proceeding to show compassion and kindness towards another fellow human being, allowing this certain homeless person to use the facilities, under certain conditions.

As you can read and hopefully get a small glimpse of the condition of Teagan's heart. Full of compassion, kindness, gentleness... all attributes of a fierce love. She wasn't perfect... very human, but when the pressure was on, she stood for what was just, what was lovely. It was the underlying, steadfast character in her that showed the truth. It was the condition of her heart. Ironically, it was the only strong, complete organ that was left of her mortal body that was donated to save someone else's life. Her dad and I chose to do this because we knew she would have wanted to help someone else.

No human can place a price or a value on another person's life. We are all very valuable to our Creator. To provide a list of how this horrific event impacted those she left behind would be unobtainable and unending. Truthfully, it would take so much negative thinking which would lead to harmful emotions and self-righteous anger... we don't want to go there. It leads to no good. The only way for a true and proper healing is to forgive. We have chosen to forgive Darius for the death of our daughter. And we want the court to know that we, The Wehrmann Family forgave Darius, just as God has forgiven us for our sins.

In conclusion, there is no possible means for restitution, but only appropriation that we request of the courts. Walt and I are in the process of building a foundation (https://thewehrmannfoundation. org/)that will serve two purposes: 1) to allow people to remember or get to know Teagan's Heart and 2) to continue her legacy of helping those in need. We want to give Darius and others the opportunity to "pay it forward." We are grateful for today, as this brings closure to this chapter in our lives and concludes this portion of Teagan's story.

Thank you,
Walt and Janette Wehrmann
Parents of Teagan R. Wehrmann

Teagan's Senior Speech

Teagan Wehrmann
Mr. Johnson
10 June 2016
English 5
Farewell/ S.E.P. Oral Presentation

The day is finally here. Graduation. We've been thinking about this day since who knows when and I remember how excited and happy I was to even think about school being over. Now, to be honest I'm scared. Many have heard the quote, "I have not failed, I've just found 10,000 ways that won't work."—Thomas Edison. The modesty of this quote has made every complexity, well what I believed to be difficult, simple and motivational. A little push to keep me going. My name is Teagan Rylee Wehrmann, and I am happy to have embarked this high school journey with those by my side.

I moved to this new city not knowing anyone and starting off with nobody by my side. Growing up with the same people for 16 years was like having a second family, then leaving the next night was hard, and I always felt alone. I started my high school years out at Corona del Mar and am finishing my last year here at Newport Harbor. The past three years have been complete chaos and like a rock in my shoe. For me, CDM was an ongoing nightmare.

Almost everything was done for image, and it was hard to fit in, especially being a German-Latina when the majority was white. When I walked on that campus, it felt that people only turned heads to throw a judgment, which is typically true. The only thing I mesmerized was the movement and ticking sound of the second, minute, and hour hands of the clocks. It felt like freedom when the minute hand reached the 12 and the bell rang. When I transferred to Newport Harbor High school, I thought that it was going to be the same, but it wasn't. As I stepped foot on this campus, I felt welcomed. If anything, the students turned heads to smile at you, compliment you, and make you feel apart of their social group, even when you didn't think you'd fit in. But that's the best thing about this place. You don't have to try and fit in. Unlike my experience at CdM, you can actually be your true self and were appreciated for it. Instead of a judgment, I would get a compliment such as "Knarley," or "Yooo respect! Teach me how to do that!" I felt that we were all an inspiration to each other, and I still have that feeling till this very day. The days I spent here only made me grow. I was supported for my successes as well as my failures. My failures include writing papers, procrastination, having high self-esteem, and finding out not who I will be, but as well as who I am. I didn't learn much from my successes as much as I did from failures, clearly since I am already advanced in that era. I succeeded in progressing my failures by not giving up. I never gave up on myself because those I surrounded myself around never gave up on me. I regretted wasting most of my year in trying to expand my social circle searching for the wrong things, when in reality, it was better for the right people to come to me, which happened to occur when I stopped searching when half the year was wasted. Wasted… I pondered over this word for days since it's getting close to the end. But that's one of the most important lessons I want to share. The time that I thought was a waste, wasn't.

It was time I used to observe, experience, and learn. Also, even though it may seem like the end, as everyone parts in their own direction, this is only the beginning. I also regretted the day I stopped motivating myself to become involved and continue in sports. I was on varsity soccer freshman year. I was supposed to get my letterman jacket as well as a scholarship, but when I moved here, I couldn't play due to CIF rules, so I discontinued out of anger. I completely messed myself over. Yet, another lesson I learned. Just because you're unable to do something for a period of time doesn't mean its stopping you forever and from continuing. After the frustration I withheld for years, I later found out that I was able to continue and could have gotten what I wanted, but it was too late. But just because it was too late, doesn't mean the offer isn't still around. As some would say, "If a door closes, another one will open." I will continue my passion next year as I move forward into college. I love the humor and positive energy that surrounds me when it comes to having a great time and spending it with friends. Much won't be mentioned because of where and how these jokes have taken place, but even the most humorous, innocent, memorable jokes that take place here in class. High school was also difficult, juggling 2 jobs, having the responsibility of not only taking care of myself but help provide for my family and be the role model of my 2-year-old niece, which was very difficult because being a teenager and having an attitude didn't work; but still managed to keep it together and having a positive attitude and expressing happiness so she will reflect upon it, as well as struggle to keep my grades high. In which I've succeeded, passing with A's and one B.

These experiences have shaped me to be who I am today. A strong, patient, kind, intelligent, motivated, passionate young woman who won't take negativity from anyone because I know where I stand, and because I know my place, I know how to respect and learn from others, which is a good quality to have in order to get somewhere in life. I also put others before myself and because of that, I gained their respect and friendship along with connections. I want to make a shout out to everybody, not only in this class but the whole school, in fact, all of society. But to keep it short and simple, I'm grateful to have the very few closest in my life, which includes my parents, my 3 brothers, William Brown, Dominic Komedia, my teachers and God. Truthfully, I've felt that my parents have never been around. They're constantly working morning to night and I don't spend much time with them unless it's a late evening and were together watching a show or movie. It was somewhat rare for all of us to be at a dinner table together. As I grow older, its like I never see them. I wake up, go to school, come home and they're gone to work, and when I leave for work, they come home and by the time I get home, everyone is asleep. I felt that my parents weren't there for me when they've really been here for me all along. I now understand that all those hours they've put in, was to provide and support me. They will always be there for me. Having them not physically being around has taught me to be independent. Me waiting for the time to talk to them when they are available has taught me patience. My parents taught me the importance of hard work, and modesty. Without that, I wouldn't have pushed myself to work and provide myself with the things I have, such as my own Mercedes and in a few months, my own home. Without this, chances are I would be feeding off my parents and honestly, I wouldn't want that. I'm happy that I wasn't one to have to rely on others. Although they weren't around or I wasn't around for them to tell me they love me, I learned to love even more because that too is what they needed. Although we're busy growing up, we forget they're growing old. They taught me that life isn't a race and to enjoy every moment I can and to love, even those with the most differences. I want to thank William Brown and Dominic Komedia because although we haven't known each other forever, or even hang out everyday, you guys taught me the importance of sticking together even through the hard times. You both are respectable gentlemen and you both taught me that I don't have to be what people expect me to be based upon where I'm from or where/how I grew up. You taught me to be content and happy with what I am given. You taught me not to give up on what I dreamed of. Like you guys said "Dreams? Nahhh, goals." I want to thank my teachers. I don't have any specifics because all of them taught me the same thing every year. Not to give up on myself. And I realize that the reason they repeat things year after year is because after a few times, "ding." Lightbulb goes on. Last but not least, I want to thank God. The big man. The reason for it all. I want to thank the Lord for being there through every struggle and every success. I want to thank Him for being the light I walk in and not by sight.

My Senior exit project was about my picky palette. I was picky about what I ate and pushing myself to try something I never would have thought about trying, and it ended up being the best thing because it turns out I really liked it. For example squid. At first I was iffy about it, but when I got the courage and went for it, it was the best thing. In a way, high school is the same. You'll never know unless you try it. For example, art. I always thought it was a waste of time and I never had the skills or patience for it, but when I took the leap and signed up for the class, I saw the talent I never thought I had. Like some of us, my future is a surprise, even for myself. Yes, I will be attending OCC for two years working towards my pre-med and then I hope to transfer to Washington State University to become a neurosurgeon. This is my dream which has become my goal. Yet again, I can't control the directions my life will go, but as I move forward, I am in control of what I do for the result of that direction. And if I mess up, I know I am able to pick myself up and continue. I will also be traveling the world, progressing my Deutsche (German), francais (French), y espanol, (and Spanish). I have arrived at these conclusions due to my experience here with all of you. Funny how freshman year to even about a month ago, I finally realized what I officially want to do, who I am, and the steps I will take to who I will become. I will miss the funny irrelevant drama that we thought was so important. I will miss sharing the laughs and joy that is brought from everyone. I will miss hearing the sound of Adriana's voice from a distance telling me to put on a sweater even on a scorching hot day. I will miss the feeling of being stoked when you pull into a parking spot a split second before some one else does. And lastly, I will miss seeing all of your beautiful faces as I walk down these halls. We all have a purpose. I hated seeing some people confess their feelings of being worthless because you weren't to me. You all made a huge impact on my life. And for me, that was everything.

In Germany, we say "Du siehst den Wald vor lauter Bäumen nicht." Meaning, you don't see the forest for all the trees.

To the class of 2016, welcome to the beginning.

THE
WEHRMANN
FOUNDATION

"...OAKS OF RIGHTEOUSNESS" ISAIAH 61:3

God takes the broken pieces of our lives and transforms
them into something beautiful. He gives beauty for ashes.
The Wehrmann Foundation was created as a tool, a means
to help provide safe places for women and children—
The will and heart of our Heavenly Father:
"A father of the fatherless and a judge *and* protector
of the widows *is* God in His holy habitation. God
places the solitary in families *and* gives the desolate
a home in which to dwell; He leads the prisoners
out to prosperity; but the rebellious dwell in a
parched land."—Psalm 68:5–6 (AMPC)

Proceeds from this book will go directly to the
foundation. To learn more visit us at:
thewehrmannfoundation.org